1975

POTTERY *The Technique of Throwing*

POTTERY *The Technique of Throwing*

John Colbeck

Photographs by Bonnie van de Wetering

B. T. Batsford Limited
Watson-Guptill Publications, New York

© John Colbeck 1969
First published 1969
Reprinted 1971
Reprinted 1974
ISBN 0 7134 2500 8
Library of Congress Catalog Card Number 69–12656

Printed and bound by
The Anchor Press Ltd, Tiptree, Essex
for the publishers
B. T. Batsford Limited
4 Fitzhardinge Street, London, W.1, and
Watson-Guptill Publications
One Astor Plaza, New York, NY 10036

Contents

Acknowledgment

As an ex-student of his my sincere and enduring thanks are due to William Newlands for the help, encouragement and instruction in throwing which he gave me.

I am grateful to Gilbert Harding-Green for encouraging me to produce this book, and to Thelma Nye for her advice during its production. Most especially I am indebted to Bonnie van de Wetering for the time and the understanding which she put into the work of taking the photographs.

J.C.   London 1969

Section 1

Introduction

Technique is only the means of achieving an aim and with throwing, as with most techniques, the aims in using the technique may be very diverse. Throwing itself is an incomplete process. It is only part of the larger process of pottery making. A thrown form to be 'finished' must at least be fired. It may, in addition, be glazed in part or in whole, and it may be treated in any one of the wealth of graphic techniques open to the potter. These facts alone make an enormous variety of end-product inevitable. But, in addition, and perhaps more important as a contributary factor to this variety, is the nature of throwing itself.

The use of throwing in pottery making is not inevitable. There are other forming techniques which have interesting possibilities. Throwing, however, is unique in that a number of forms may be made quickly which vary slightly or greatly. Virtually identical forms can be made by throwing but in this it is not a unique technique. (Slip casting, for example, produces virtually identical forms more exactly and, in an industrial context, more quickly than throwing, but obviously it results in forms of a different quality.) Released from his traditional social responsibility of making standardised articles for everyday use, the modern thrower will probably be more interested in exploring the immense variety of possible forms.

Whatever the nature of the finished result the concern of the thrower must, at some level, have been with the creation of three-dimensional form —with the nature of the details of edges, with surface, with convexity and concavity, and, obviously, with the nature of the overall form. However an object is finished, what is done at the throwing stage determines much of its final nature. The techniques involved in making objects of the same family of form, however diverse their appearance or use, are very similar.

The technique of using a potters wheel may be divided into two main techniques and a small number of processes, the two techniques being throwing and turning. Turning is not inevitably a part of the process but when used it always follows throwing.

It is the aim of this book to show and describe these two techniques and the main procedures related to them.

Throwing is the process of shaping an even mass of soft plastic clay by hand on a wheelhead revolving at speeds varied by the thrower.

Turning is the process of paring away excess clay from a leather-hard form.

It is a not uncommon belief that throwing is difficult, but if the problems are approached purposefully and methodically and if the processes are understood a worthwhile standard should be achieved by anyone who devotes sufficient time to practice. Practice is essential to acquire technique and to become acquainted with and to understand materials. Clay is a substance which can vary enormously both in its nature and, for any given clay, in its consistency, i.e. its water content. Acquiring a deep knowledge of clay is a far lengthier process than learning the techniques of throwing.

Section 2

Clay

All clays do not lend themselves equally well to the process of throwing. 'Plasticity' is too limited a term to describe their relevant qualities, as 'plasticity' can be as correctly applied to clays which have very limited throwing qualities as it can to good throwing clays. The coined words 'throwable' and 'throwability' are more specific.

There are several qualities which make clays good for throwing.

1 They should be plastic in the broad sense of the word in that they are readily formable.
2 They should, in addition, not absorb water too quickly and hence soften and become coated in a thick layer of slip.
3 They should be rigid enough to retain whatever form they are thrown into, though obviously there are limits, without either sagging or cracking when throwing is completed.

The fact that a clay may be plastic when it is coiled or rolled into sheets and placed into moulds does not necessarily mean that it is a good throwing clay.

An excellent chapter on 'Clay and Pottery Bodies' in Dora Billington's book, *The Technique of Pottery*, gives a lucid description of clays and of their blending. Let it suffice here to say that the purer primary clays tend to be poorer throwing bodies and that the impurer secondary clays tend to be good throwing clays.

Any clay can be mixed with any other clay to achieve a compromise of qualities, and non-plastic materials may also be added. All blending and additions will alter to some extent the working and the fired qualities of clays. Ball clay, in quite large proportions, bentonite, usually in very small proportions (less than 6%), are the most usual additions when increased plasticity is required. Clean silver sand and grog can both be added to throwing clays and can reduce the tendency of a clay to sag. All additions to clay should be fully recorded and tested and it should be remembered that the fired quality of a clay is arguably of greater importance than its working qualities. One of the challenges of all creative processes is working within the limits set by materials and techniques.

Clearly, however, a beginner's task will be facilitated by good throwing clays. These are generally available from clay merchants found in clay mining areas and in most large cities. Firms supplying schools and art schools have a wider and often more suitable selection than those supplying the industry. There are four main possibilities, each capable of a variety of qualities.

1 Red earthenware clays which are, on the whole, excellent throwing bodies.
2 Refined fireclay bodies, often with added sand and ball clay, are usually good.
3 Buff earthenware and stoneware bodies are sometimes good but are more variable.
4 White bodies are generally poor throwing clays.

Clays of any of the first three groups are suitable for beginners. However strongly an individual is drawn to the whiteness of white clays, they should be avoided to start with as they will usually only hamper learning. Using white clay is, moreover, not the only way of making a white object.

Ideally the beginner should mainly use a good clay while techniques are being learned, but should frequently try as many clays as are available so that the differing qualities of clays may from the start be appreciated and the necessary adjustments to them be understood and applied. This appreciation of the differing natures of various clays is essential to the full development of throwing techniques.

Whatever clay has been chosen the most essential process prior to actual throwing is the preparation of the clay.

The aim of preparing clay is to make it into a homogenous mass of totally even consistency. The process of throwing, which is essentially evenly squeezing the revolving walls of a form, becomes totally nonsensical if the clay itself is uneven because the even pressure of the hands will affect soft clay more than hard clay, making the softer parts thinner and an eccentric wobbly form will develop which will almost always collapse.

The mixing of clay effected in a pug-mill is insufficient and even if one is available, and new clay is being used, it should be thoroughly prepared by hand before it is thrown. There are various ways of doing this.

Many beginners have the mistaken belief that throwing is difficult, but their problem is due far more to their bad preparation of the clay than to any problems inherent in the techniques of throwing. Though this book is about throwing, some space is devoted to clay preparation because of its vital importance.

All the photographs in this section show the mixing of a dark clay with a light clay simply to clarify the process. Though this, in practice, may only rarely be done, doing it a few times should both acquaint beginners with what happens and the time it takes to happen, for with mixing clays of two colours the point when they are totally blended can be seen.

All the manual mixing processes involve spreading the clay into a wider mass and then, by some means, returning it to a taller mass and then again spreading it.

1 Before mixing clay by any process it is a good idea to divide the mass into two halves and to cut each half into a number of layers. These layers are then interleaved. This should give an even distribution of any unevennesses present

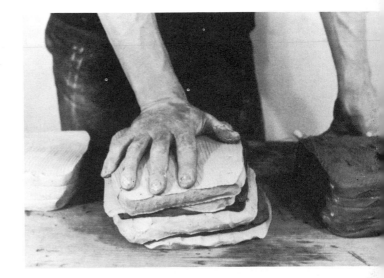

Wedging

Wedging consists of cutting a clay mass in half, throwing one half down on to the other, which spreads the mass out to its previous size, and repeating this process for quite a number of times until the clay is even.

2 The clay is cut into two pieces

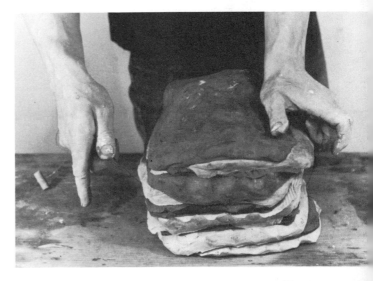

3 The cut mass shows the layers

4 The two pieces are forcibly thrown together

5 In practice when the two halves have been thrown together one end is pressed down and the other lifted up to facilitate cutting

6 After only a very few cutting and throwing down actions considerable mixing can be seen to have taken place

The process continues until evenness is achieved. After each throwing down action it is a good idea to firmly tap the edges of the mass so that protruding pieces do not trap air in the mass.

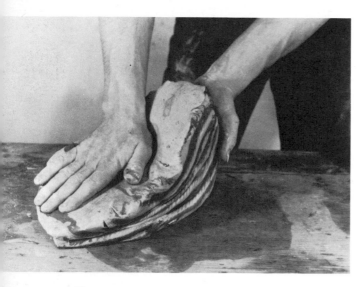

Kneading

Of the two methods of kneading described the first is probably the more quickly learned but the second, once learned, is the easier for kneading very large pieces of clay.

7 Both hands have just pushed down forcibly on the clay, maximum pressure being exerted at the wrist

8 The clay is lifted at its front end and the hands move forward on it

9 The hands begin a new downward and forward pushing motion

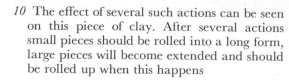

10 The effect of several such actions can be seen on this piece of clay. After several actions small pieces should be rolled into a long form, large pieces will become extended and should be rolled up when this happens

11 A section through the roll shows how the clay is being mixed

12, 13 The roll is then kneaded in its length

These actions, both the pushing down and rocking action and the rolling up of clay to change direction, should be repeated till the clay is even.

Spiral kneading

A full verbal description of spiral kneading would be very lengthy and might lead to confusion rather than clarity. It is a knack which some find very difficult to acquire. Once acquired it is probably the easiest and the most efficient way of mixing clay.

The right hand does most of the work, pushing down on the clay mass as it is rolled forward. The left hand merely contains the sideways movement of clay and creates the spiral movement by rocking the clay in a circle.

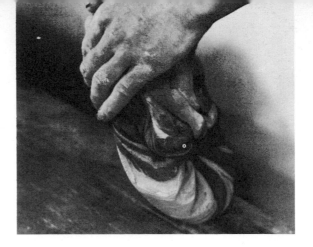

14 The beginning of the downward action

15 Halfway through the downward action the right hand is on top of the clay and has not yet exerted pressure

16 Identical position to *15* but with the left hand removed

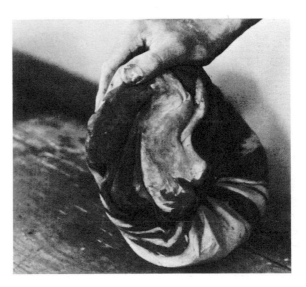

17

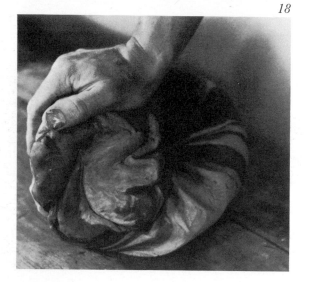

18

17 Just before the bottom of the downward movement the right hand is above the thickest mass of clay

18 Identical position but with the left hand removed

19 At the bottom of the downward movement the wrist and palm of the right hand exert a fairly sudden downward pressure. The left hand merely contains the end of the clay mass

20 Identical position but with the left hand removed

19

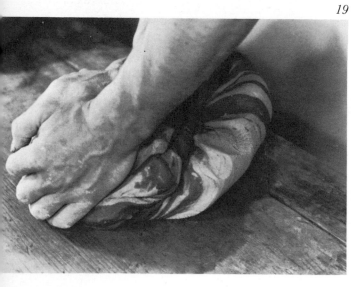

20

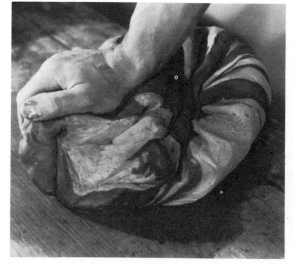

16

21 The left hand lifts and pivots the clay. The right hand moves forward in relation to the left to what will become at the beginning of the next movement the highest point

22 The right hand continues the lifting action as the left hand pivots to its new position. The clay returns to the position shown in *14* for the start of a new movement

Once learned spiral kneading can be done in an easy rhythmic movement.

23 The form of the mass of clay during spiral kneading

24 A section shows the considerable, complex mixing taking place

21

22

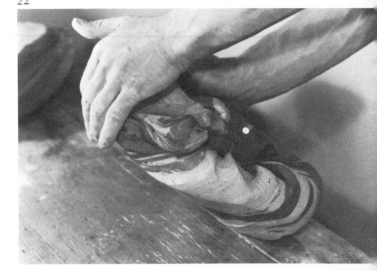

24

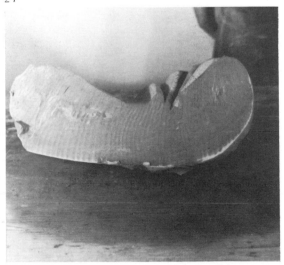

23

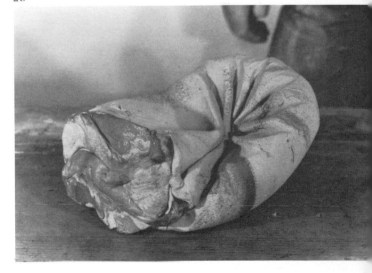

Probably the quickest mixing process of all is to wedge clay and then spirally knead it but any of these three processes can be combined in any order.

A quick way to mix a small amount of clay is to repeatedly halve and throw together a lump of clay in the hands.

A good guide as to whether clay is even is to cut a lump in half and to throw it down on a bench so the cut edge is vertical. If the pressure of throwing down distorts the cut edge into a ridged texture, the softer clay being forced outwards, then unevenness is considerable. If the cut edge remains smooth then the clay is probably even but the kind of gently grading unevenness which exists in clay which has been stored will not show.

There is, in fact, no way of determining whether clay is even except by acquired experience.

Once the technique of spiral kneading has been learned very large amounts of clay can be prepared. The limit to the amount of clay which can be prepared as one piece is determined by the consistency of the clay and strength of the individual. Co-ordination is, however, of greater importance than strength and strength alone need not be a limiting factor as larger pieces of clay than can be kneaded at one time can be made even by kneading small amounts separately then wedging them into one mass, dividing the mass and re-kneading it in separate pieces and finally re-wedging it as one mass.

Wedging and kneading should both make the clay air free. Air bubbles can be a considerable inconvenience in a thrown wall of clay but, during firing are not as disastrous as is sometimes thought.

Wood, slate and marble are all good surfaces on which to knead. Plaster is to be avoided.

Clay will not stay even for long periods. Clay preparation should ideally immediately precede throwing and prepared clay should be wrapped in polythene (polyethylene).

Simply being exposed to air or resting on a slightly porous surface, such as wood, can cause unevennesses to develop surprisingly quickly.

Prepared clay should be cut and then beaten into neat roughly spherical forms as it is put into polythene (polyethylene). This will greatly facilitate the initial stages of throwing.

Plenty of clay should be prepared. Nothing helps learning as much as correcting failures and repeating successes immediately.

Section 3

Wheels

A throwing wheel, very simply, is a machine designed to rotate a round turntable in a horizontal plane at readily variable speeds on a constant vertical axis.

Historically, throwing wheels being so simple in principle have taken very diverse forms and have been powered in many different ways. Today kick wheels and electric wheels are the two common types of wheel but exist in too large a variety of forms to describe them all here.

The three main types of kick wheel in current use are the front treadle type, the side treadle type and the type where the thrower kicks directly on to the flywheel.

The front treadle type, though usually sturdily made has generally only a light flywheel. It is virtually useless for throwing or turning large forms and is somewhat tiring to throw anything on for long periods but is just about serviceable for turning where a standardised production of small objects is undertaken. Provision of a seat is neither usual nor convenient on this type. As a general purpose wheel this type is very limiting.

The side treadle wheel and the type kicked directly, providing they are sturdily constructed and have a heavy flywheel are both excellent machines. If the flywheel is too light, centring speed will be tiring to maintain and the steadiness of the slow speeds necessary for finishing will be poor. Flywheels can be too heavy which makes them exhausting to move at speed and difficult to stop. Systems of increasing and decreasing the weight of a flywheel are a good idea when a variety of people use a wheel for a wide variety of size of forms.

The side treadle type are more expensive than the front treadle type but both are cheaper than electric wheels. The direct kicking type can only be made. All kick wheels are considerably simpler than electric to make. A kick wheel is free to operate in terms of money alone.

Electric wheels use a variety of systems to transfer the rotation of the motor to the wheelhead and to vary the speed of the rotation. In function, electric wheels fall into two categories —those designed for industrial use and those designed for non-industrial use. The main difference is the speed of rotation, but industrial wheels do tend to be somewhat heavier. Industrial throwing is limited to the throwing stage of 'throwing and turning' (see Section 8) which being thicker can be done at speeds of rotation considerably in excess of those suitable for non-industrial throwing.

Reducing the speed of any wheel is a relatively simple matter but is only of use if sufficient width of speed range is not lost. All electric wheels have a foot-operated lever to vary the speed of rotation. On non-industrial wheels a notching system usually accompanies this lever allowing the speed to be set in a number of positions between maximum and minimum speed. A minimum speed of not more than 50 r.p.m. and a maximum of not much less than 130 r.p.m. are essential in an electric wheel intended for throwing of all sizes and types. It should be impossible to slow down the rotation of the wheel by manual pressure on the wheelhead both at maximum and minimum speeds and with any reasonable weight of clay.

Seats are invariably incorporated into industrial wheels. On non-industrial wheels they are usually standard 'extras'.

A good kick wheel and a good electric wheel are comparably efficient machines for the throwing of small and medium sized forms.

For the centring, throwing and finishing of large and very large forms a good electric wheel is an arguably better machine. An assistant to do the kicking is often necessary if very tall forms are to be made on a kick wheel.

Though both electric and kick wheels are

simple machines it is very important that their moving parts are well maintained. Regular greasing is neither a time consuming nor a lengthy process. Specially regular attention should be paid to the top and bottom bearings. Bad maintenance leads to a noisy, inefficient machine and eventually to sometimes surprisingly expensive repairs or replacements. Given proper attention the moving metal parts of a wheel should virtually last forever. Being somewhat more complex electric wheels generally need more maintenance than kick wheels.

Whatever the type of wheel the wheelhead is usually attached to the shaft in one of two ways either by a threaded screw fit or by a taper fit. On non-industrial wheels, both kick and electric, the taper fit type is the more common.

25 With the wheelhead removed most wheels look something like this. The tapered end of the shaft protrudes through the top bearing and is surrounded by a deep tray in rigid plastic or galvanised iron to catch the water, slip and clay discarded from the wheel during throwing. This tray must be rigid enough to allow considerable pressure to be exerted on it. The tray is surmounted by a rubber or copper edge to give a more comfortable surface on which to rest and brace the arms. The tray is generally drained of water and slip through a hose which is fitted with a plug. The tray must never be allowed to fill to anything like a depth which would allow water or slip to cover the top edge of the top bearing. The wooden ledge is standard on most wheels and is used as a convenient surface on which to place a bowl of water, tools, wire and sponges. If the galvanised surface gets chipped and starts to rust the whole tray should be cleaned, rubbed down and painted with a good bitumen or lead paint. The varnish with which the wooden ledge is usually treated is very short lived and when it has worn off, if the wood is treated occasionally with a good beeswax-based polish, it will both be preserved and be easier to wipe clean than if left untreated

26 A variety of sizes of wheelhead is available. Wheelheads of the taper fit type are placed in position simply by locating the end of the shaft in the recessed hole under the wheelhead. They are removed by a sharply twisting, slightly rising action, gripping the wheelhead with both hands while the wheel is stationary. Wheelheads should be regularly removed and left off the machine when not in use. If left on for long periods they tend to become partially rusted on and are very difficult to remove. Both the hole in the wheelhead and the end of the shaft should be kept rust free, if necessary by the use of oil. If oil is used to excess the wheelhead will slip on the shaft, and the shaft and the hole in the wheelhead will have to be wiped dry of oil

27 One of the problems of throwing is in removing thin wet clay forms from the wheelhead. One good solution to this is to fix two metal studs into the wheelhead and to have a quantity of round asbestos bats drilled with corresponding holes. The studs should protrude from the wheelhead no farther than the minimum thickness of the bats used. No additional fixing of the bats is necessary

28 It is useful to have some bats as large as will fit in the wheel tray

29 A fairly wide wheelhead is best if throwing is to be done directly on it. Most metal wheelheads are lightly grooved on their machined upper surface

30 It is perfectly possible to fix bats to a wheelhead with clay alone. Asbestos, wood, plaster of paris and occasionally terracotta bats are used. A thin layer of clay is centred and spread out on the wheelhead roughly to the diameter of the bat, it is grooved with the fingers and sponged with water. Wood and asbestos bats need only be sponged with a damp sponge but plaster and terracotta bats need sponging with sufficient water to reduce extreme porosity. The porosity of terracotta bats will vary depending on the temperature of firing and the type of clay. Non-porous bats of any material do not stick well to clay. It is impossible to stick waterlogged plaster bats on to clay and equally impossible to get throwing clay to stick on top. If plaster bats are too dry they harden throwing clay rapidly and make the base of forms difficult to throw and cut off with control. Judging the right degree of dampness for plaster bats is quickly learned with experience

31 The dampened bat is pushed on to the dampened and grooved clay. If its porosity is right it will quickly stick and should remain firmly stuck for a considerable time

32 When throwing has been finished the bat can be gently levered off with a flat wooden tool. This will require very little pressure but the hand not levering should steady the bat preventing it suddenly jerking up

Plaster bats should be round edged to avoid the danger of chipping and when used the use of metal tools should be avoided.

Plaster top surfaces are sometimes cast onto metal or wooden wheelheads as a permanent working surface. Unless one has strong personal reasons for preferring this it should be avoided. There is, as with plaster bats, the danger of contaminating the clay with plaster. A stronger reason is that once the plaster is waterlogged clay will not stick to it and the wheelhead has to be allowed to dry before further throwing can be done.

During all throwing processes, with one or two possible exceptions, the clay wall being formed should revolve through the hands, passing the wrists first, rather than into the hands, passing the fingertips first. As the clay revolves through the hands a gentler more controllable pressure is possible than if it revolves into the hands.

Thus with a wheel revolving anti-clockwise the right-hand side of a form is worked on, right hand outside, left hand inside. If the wheel revolves clockwise the situation is exactly reversed: the left-hand side of the form is worked on with the right hand inside and the left hand outside.

Anti-clockwise is by far the more usual direction of rotation for throwing wheels. Electric wheels always, unless altered or specially ordered, revolve anti-clockwise: users of kick wheels invariably throw with the wheel revolving anti-clockwise.

Should for any reason a clockwise direction be preferred and there is no reason why not, all actions are the exact mirror opposite of all the photographs in this book which were all taken of throwing on an electric wheel revolving in a conventional anti-clockwise direction.

Section 4

Centring

The first step in learning to throw is to learn to centre the clay quickly and efficiently.

The object of centring is to make the clay revolve centrally on the wheelhead so that when subsequently it is opened up the walls are immediately of constant thickness in horizontal section and are of even height. The finished form of a centred lump of clay will be related in width to the type and size of form being made.

Throughout the centring process, as in all throwing processes the entire surface of the clay is lubricated with water. A bowl of water should be kept constantly at hand, so that the hands and the clay may be kept wet.

Centring is done by the logical application of steady firm pressures on the surface of the revolving piece of clay. No great amount of strength is necessary.

The ball of clay should be a neat homogenous mass and should be firmly placed in the centre of the wheelhead or bat which should be dampened with a wet sponge. The neater this ball of clay is and the closer it is placed to the centre, the quicker and the easier will be the centring process.

A common centring hold and the basic pressures involved are here demonstrated on a small and a medium sized piece of clay.

33, 37 There should be no difficulty in placing smaller pieces of clay centrally on the wheel which can be immediately set in motion. Before either the hands or clay are dampened it is as well with medium sized pieces to check that they are centrally placed and of fairly even form. Any unevennesses should be pushed or tapped until the clay is fairly symmetrical

Two main pressures tend to centre the rotating mass of clay:

35, 40 A downward vertical pressure. This pressure is most easily applied by the outside edge of the palm of the right hand. The forearm points to the centre of the wheel and is steadied by resting on the edge of the wheel tray. This pressure exerted alone tends to displace the clay into a wider form

36

35

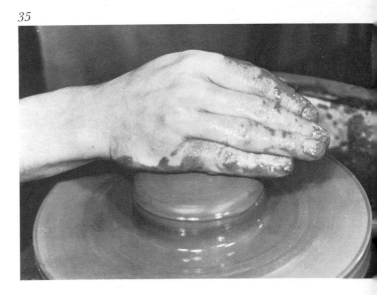

37

38

36, 38 An inward horizontal pressure. This pressure is most easily exerted by the wrist end of the palm of the left hand. This forearm also points to the centre of the wheel and is steadied by resting on the edge of the wheel tray. This pressure exerted alone tends to displace the clay into a taller form

In practice these two pressures are only rarely applied singly. Small and medium sized pieces can generally be centred by the simultaneous application of the two pressures.

34 , 39 The two pressures isolated in the two previous pairs of photographs are here shown combined. Every opportunity should be taken while centring of achieving additional steadiness through contact of the hands with each other

39

40

There are other centring holds than the one illustrated. All involve an application of the same two pressures.

41 Here the thumbs alone exert the downward pressure while the wrist end of both palms push steadily on the side of the clay

42 Here again the thumbs and the wrist ends of both palms exert the two pressures but the basic movement here is a pulling action

In both these holds, as in the previous hold, additional steadiness is achieved by contact between the hands and by resting the forearms on the edge of the wheel tray.

Pressure either downwards or inwards should not be suddenly released. As the clay passes through the hands it is being continually displaced. If the pressure causing this displacement is removed suddenly an unevenness will become evident which was not before present. Pressure during all stages of throwing should be gradually released.

When the form of a centred piece of clay needs adjusting to either a wider or a taller shape it should be adjusted by the application of a greater and a lesser pressure not by some pressure and no pressure. The hand exerting lesser pressure contains the clay displaced by the greater pressure and prevents it developing unevenness which would otherwise tend to occur.

A process often used by throwers making large numbers of objects quickly is to squeeze the clay up into a tall cone and then down into a flatter form and to repeat this up and down action two or three times before commencing actual throwing.

This is a mixing process rather than a centring process—the clay is in fact centred almost immediately. The procedure is left over from the days before polythene (polyethylene) when clay was stored in wet sacking resting probably on wood. Where the clay touched the sack it would become damper and where it was on wood or exposed it would dry slightly. This squeezing up and down will eliminate slight unevenness but should not be used to try to eliminate the kind of unevenness which exists in unprepared clay.

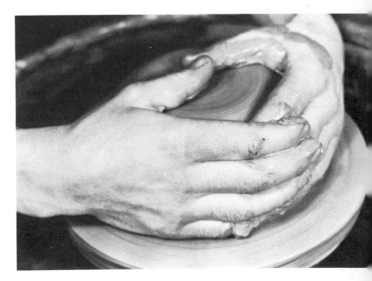

43, 44 Both hands push firmly on the clay. The containing action of the thumbs is only slight and the clay is allowed to rise into a taller form

45, 46 The palms of the hands apply pressure on opposite sides of the clay and simultaneously rise, shaping the clay into a tall conical form

47, 48 The right hand pivots up on to the top of the clay form and exerts a firm downward pressure. The inward pressure of the left hand is still very firm and is sufficient to prevent the clay mushrooming out at the top but slight enough to allow the clay to be displaced downwards and outwards into a lower wider form. The steadying action of the right hand fingers which firmly rest on the back of the left hand is an important part of the downward motion of the hands

This cycle of movements can be repeated until unevenness is no longer suspected. The form should be convex at the top from the start of the squeezing, upward motion otherwise it can develop a hollow centre trapping slip and water in the middle and making the clay unthrowable. It is very important that mushrooming out does not develop during the downward motion as this also can cause slip and water to be trapped in the mass of the clay.

The distinct lean noticeable in *46* and *47* is quite normal. During both centring actions and this mixing process the clay can be round and centred but may, where a horizontal pressure is being applied, not be revolving on the same vertical axis as the wheel.

If the pressure illustrated in *46* or *47* was suddenly released the clay would swing in an even circle as wide as the extent of its displacement from the centre of the wheel when pressure was released.

All pressures during centring, this mixing process, opening out and throwing should be gradually released. The fact that during throwing processes the clay may be displaced from a centred position on the wheel but still be under perfect control is simply part of the nature of plasticity and is one of the qualities which enables it to be thrown in such diverse forms without loss of control.

A truly centred piece of clay is the essential beginning to throwing any controlled form however large or small.

Section 5

Opening

When the clay has been centred the next step is to make a depression in the centre. The clay thus ceases to be an evenly revolving mass and becomes an evenly revolving wall. This wall is later thinned to a greater or lesser extent.

The functions of the opening process are to determine the inside form, thickness and width of the thrown base and to create the initial wall form.

Whether the form is to be subsequently turned or not, the most important lesson to learn in opening up a centred clay form is to gauge the thickness of clay left in the base. If too little thickness of clay is left in the base, the wire used to cut the thrown form off the bat or wheelhead may rise up right through the base or leave it too thin. If too much clay is left in the base the form will be unintentionally heavy or will require excessive turning. Gauging the thickness of clay left in the base is a knack which should be fairly easy to acquire quickly. It should be possible to feel the thickness by placing one hand on the bat surface and one hand on the clay surface. Equally it should be possible to see the difference. With practice, judgment through both these senses can become extremely accurate. A test which can be used to develop the accuracy of tactile or visual judgment of thickness is to hold a long needle set in a cork farther from its end than the clay thickness can possibly be, to push the needle vertically into the clay until it stops on the bat or wheelhead surface, to slide the fingers down the needle until they touch the clay surface, to grip the needle and withdraw it. The distance from the fingers to the end of the needle is, obviously, the thickness of the clay.

One point which should be remembered is that the actual thickness of clay is never the thickness left in the base after the thrown form has been cut off. A wire, however tightly it is held as it is passed under the thrown form always slightly reduces the thickness of its base because some clay is always left on the bat or wheelhead. Three factors concerning the behaviour of a wire when a form is cut off its bat are relevant here. Firstly, the thicker the wire used to cut off a form the higher it will rise into the clay of the base. Secondly, the harder the clay being cut off the higher the wire will rise and thirdly the wider the clay form the higher the wire will rise into the middle of the base of the form.

The initial wall is created automatically as soon as a hollow is made in the centred form of clay. The thickness, width and form of the base will vary, being dependent on the intention of the thrower and the type of form being made.

Once the wall of a thrown form has been thinned to any great extent further adjustment to the thickness of the base is almost impossible. The opening process therefore determines the thickness and form of the base fairly irrevocably and determines its width too, but within slightly more flexible limits.

The eventual aim should be to complete the opening process determining all the relevant aspects of the inside base in one action.

There are various ways of depressing the middle of a centred form of clay. Each person will probably evolve variations of his own. Various methods can also be combined.

Personal preference for the speed of revolution of the wheel will be developed with experience.

The consistency and type of clay, being used and the form being opened will both affect any decision about slowing down the wheel. Opening can usually be done at much the same speed of revolution as centring. Soft clay may require a reduction in speed.

Two common methods are demonstrated. These are relevant with slight variations in practice from the very smallest scale up to a scale where they cease to be convenient to the individual.

49, 51 The thumbs supporting each other make an initial insertion into the centre of the revolving clay

49

50

51

52

53

50, 52, 53 The thumbs push downwards and move away from the body shaping the base to the required thickness, width and form. The increase in width which the outward movement of the thumbs tends to create is prevented or controlled by the fingers and especially the palm of the left hand. The upward movement of the displaced clay prevented from moving outwards is contained between the thumb and palm of the left hand

54, 56 The fingers of the right hand push down in the centre of the revolving clay making an initial insertion

54

55

55, 57, 58 Moving downwards initially and then away from the centre towards the left hand the fingers of the right hand shape the base to the required thickness, width and form. The left hand contains and controls the outward and upward movement of displaced clay between thumb and palm

In the first method the left forearm is steadied by resting on the edge of the wheel tray. In the second method both forearms can rest on the wheel tray edge. It should be noticed that throughout both movements both hands are firmly linked. The additional steadiness achieved by this is of great importance.

It will not always be possible, certainly at first, to create a base of exactly the thickness, width and form required. Subsequent shaping movements identical to the two opening movements shown can be used until the base is as required. It is of the utmost importance that during any such movements a small subsidiary wall of displaced clay is not allowed to form. If allowed to form this secondary wall may be pushed out against the initial wall trapping slip, water and possibly air and making the wall unthrowable. The main downward outward pressure in subsequent opening movements, however that pressure is applied, should be simultaneously accompanied by a slighter downward pressure effective at a point farther from the centre than the main pressure. Spreading this pressure over an area so that a radial line rather than a point is being worked on has the same preventative effect and is equally effective in changing the form. A brief look at photograph *317* should clarify this point.

The first of the two illustrated methods of opening is probably the quicker, the second method the more easily controlled and therefore perhaps the more accurate. A common practice is to use the first initially and to change to the second for finally defining the shape. In both cases it should be noticed the opening in the initial stage is at an angle of about 45 degrees and only later becomes more vertical. This allows the inside form to be more easily seen and the base thickness and width are more easily altered in subsequent opening actions without the formation of an unwanted subsidiary wall.

56

57

58

Section 6

Throwing

Throwing is the process of evenly squeezing the walls of an opened out mass of centred clay between the fingers and rising both hands together at an even speed. There are usually two distinct parts to the process, thinning the walls and shaping them.

The pressure effected on the walls of the form by the squeezing rising action of the hands and by the rotating motion of the wheel is a gradual spiral. The pressure should commence right at the bottom of the form and should continue right to the top where the hands cease rising and steady the edge before releasing pressure. The walls of the form and the hands should be sufficiently well-lubricated with water to enable each upward movement to be completed from bottom to top without removing the hands. Should the hands or clay become dry when the walls are thin the sudden friction caused by unlubricated pressure can either drag the whole form off centre or create a bulge. When dryness can be seen or felt or when some types of narrow-necked forms are being made the hands will have to be removed from the form before an upward movement has been completed. In doing this the utmost care should be taken to release pressure gently for during both thinning and shaping movements the form may be eccentric at a given point in time in much the same way as a clay mass may lean during centring and yet still be perfectly under control.

The pressures at work during the thinning process can perhaps be best demonstrated by throwing a small form between the thumb and fingers of the right hand.

59 The wall formed by opening out is gripped between the thumb and either one or both of the first two fingers. The thumb starts where the flat base becomes the wall; the fingers start where the clay meets the bat

60 Squeezing the clay firmly and constantly the thumb and fingers steadily rise up the wall

61 The squeezing rising action continues to the top of the wall. The thumb and fingers stop at the top and release pressure horizontally the thumb moving inwards, the fingers outwards. The right forearm rests on the edge of the wheel throughout this action. The aim of the action should be to thin the clay and make it gain height fairly quickly. The direction of upward movement should also be controllable

Beginners often find doing this one-handed action easier than immediately using two hands. In practice, however, the action is never or only very rarely, used.

When using two hands there are a number of ways of holding the fingers while throwing. The principle of squeezing the clay and rising the hands remains constant, however varied may be the actual application of pressure.

The position of the left hand inside a form is less easy to show than that of the outside hand. The effective point of pressure can be varied to suit a given form or simply to suit preference. In practice the most usual ways of effecting pressure on the inside wall are with the ball of the index finger or the ball of the second finger or both or with the side of the index finger. On large forms all fingers of the left hand are often used during initial thinning.

Three common positions for the right hand during the thinning of small forms are illustrated. There are obviously further possibilities.

35

62 The ball of the index finger of the left hand pushes outwards against the side of the index finger of the right hand which pushes inwards with equal pressure. The pressure is not great

63 The fingers rise simultaneously

64 Pressure ceases at the top

65 The ball of the index finger of the left hand
   pushes outwards against the bent second joint
   of the index finger of the right hand which
   pushes inwards with equal pressure

66 The fingers rise simultaneously

67 Pressure ceases at the top

68, 69, 70 The clay is squeezed between the index finger and any one of the first three fingers of the right hand. This method is used much less frequently than the previous two but beginners do find it useful for gaining additional steadiness. Two variations are possible; if the pressure inside is applied by the ball of the index finger the main pressure can be applied by any one of the fingers and can be varied, the fingers not applying pressure outside can exert a slight steadying pressure to control the form either above or below the main point of pressure; or, if the side of the index finger is used inside pressure can be spread through all three fingers, the point of main pressure usually being in the lowest finger outside and the ball of the inside finger

What happens in all these three instances is the same. The pressure is applied initially at the bottom and is then moved up the form evenly to the top. At the very beginning of the process the outside finger has to move up the form the thickness of the base before it is applying pressure in the same horizontal plane as the inside fingers. Not realising this is one reason why beginners often have difficulty thinning a wall vertically. Conscientiously keeping their hands in the same relative position they begin a rising action but because the inside hand is higher the wall is forced outwards, apparently inexplicably.

The simple thinning action should be practised until some control over the form in which the wall rises and some confidence has been achieved.

With small forms the arms can be braced on the edge of the wheeltray throughout the thinning action. This should give additional steadiness as should any direct contact between the two hands.

The steady squeezing rising action is the basic process of throwing. It is varied to produce different forms and surfaces and it affects different clays and different sizes of form differently. Once the basic process has been mastered all else, technically, will follow with practice and experience.

The desire to and the intention of learning to throw presupposes an interest in form.

Thrown forms must of necessity have some area of base and must of necessity be round in horizontal section. Such forms can develop in three basic directions: upwards vertically, outwards away from their central axis, inwards towards their central axis and in combinations of these directions.

The beginner should practise on these basic variations and combinations of forms to understand how the basic thinning process is varied and how shaping actions are done.

Vertical forms: cylinders

The cylinder is basic to an enormous variety of forms. But, contrary to some belief all forms cannot be developed from cylinders.

An initial technical aim should be to throw a form in three upward thinning movements.

71 Opening out should give the form an even flat base with as right-angular a bottom inside corner as the fingers allow

72 More control over form may be possible if the initial thinning produces a form slightly narrower at the top than the base. The even speed of the rising action is evidenced in the evenly spaced spiral of slip on the surface

73 The second thinning action also produces an evenly spaced spiral and increases the width of the top. The third thinning action begins, as should all others, right at the base of the form. The finger pushes inwards and upwards at the very base. The inside finger is held very steady till the outside finger has risen the thickness of the base

74 The two hands then rise simultaneously

75 A confident final thinning · action should result in as even a spiral as previous thinning actions and in a basically cylindrical form

76, 77 The growth of the cylinder at each stage of thinning should be a positive growth from the previous stage. The temptation of over-thinning the top of the wall in the early stages should be avoided. A wall thinned in a series of even stages will be a wall of much more even consistency than one which is tapered early on. Early thinning of the top means the top becomes softer and this can be a serious limitation both on subsequent thinning of the lower walls and on shaping

For all but the smallest forms bracing the arms on the edge of the wheel tray is impossible except at the centring, opening and initial thinning stages. Steadiness can be gained by bracing the body against the wheel and possibly in addition holding one or both of the elbows against the body. No position is steady if it is too tense. A relaxed steadiness should be possible without holding either arm against the body if the body itself is steady.

Steadiness of hand, however it is achieved, is essential in all stages of throwing.

To explain the difference between the thinning and shaping pressures in throwing, an analogy may be helpful. Imagine that a small flat piece of plastic clay about $2'' \times 3'' \times \frac{1}{2}''$ has been dipped in water and placed on a table. Try initially, with wet hands to pick up this clay and hold it without thinning it, then by squeezing to thin it to half its thickness. The pressure required to pick up the clay and hold it is closely similar to the pressure used during shaping actions—firm and steady but non-thinning. The second pressure is obviously parallel to the pressure used during thinning—stronger and firm and steady.

The rudiments of shaping can be usefully learnt by making slight adjustments to cylindrical forms.

If a cylinder needs widening at any point the shaping action should begin right at the bottom rising over the surface as steadily and definitely as thinning actions. The movement should leave the form unaffected where it is correct and should describe a truely vertical movement leaving those parts of the form which were too narrow placed in a new wider diameter. Providing this action is not rushed and providing the clay is not too thin or too soft this action should present no difficulties. If it does it should be tried on cylinders thrown evenly but thicker than usual.

If a cylinder has become too wide at the top the same shaping action should be tried this time with the intention of narrowing the form. If the clay is firm and the wall not too thin the action may be successful. The likelihood is, however, that the action will not be successful and may create folding in the top edge. An alternative is to try a method described later—collaring—whereby forms are narrowed by putting both hands around a form, fingers and thumbs describing a rough circle, and gently pushing inwards. This method may succeed where the other failed but it too may produce wobbling, folding and general unevenness.

The conclusion which can be drawn from this is perhaps the most important fact in shaping thrown walls of clay—it is far easier to increase the diameter of a thinned clay form than it is to decrease it.

One other characteristic of the behaviour of thrown clay walls should be mentioned before further forms are discussed. If an evenly thrown cylinder is shaped into a full spherical shape the walls when cut in section will where the diameter of the form has doubled be found to be still rather more than half the thickness of the walls where the diameter is unaffected. Any amount more

than half is more than would be logically expected.

This phenomenon is explicable only in terms of the nature of the clay: it is one of the qualities of plasticity. The phenomenon is obviously accompanied by a loss of height. The reverse of the phenomenon is not the exact opposite: a thrown wall collared to half its diameter is usually very nearly twice as thick but this is usually accompanied by a slight gain in height.

Forms can, however, be shaped so far from their thinned form that they become too thin and collapse.

The standard practice for throwing full forms is to thin a form taller and narrower than the intended shape and then without further thinning and in one or more shaping actions to throw the form into the wider lower.shape. Thinning forms directly to an intended shape is possible but the use of distinct thinning and shaping processes, once the limits are understood, gives a much finer degree of control of final shape.

Open forms

Forms of this type are rarely only thrown. Unless the form is only very slightly wider at the top than the bottom or has a completely flat inside base, some turning will usually be done. Most usually the inside form of open forms will describe a single uninterrupted concavity but this is not necessary.

78 The opening up creates a slight concavity in the solid base. Initial thinning can be fairly vertical

79 After the second thinning the form is of outward sloping shape

80, 81 The third, final thinning, increases both the height and the width of the form

82 Subsequent shaping actions progressively widen the form causing some loss of height

83

84

83, 84 The initial technical aim should be to thin the form in three actions and to shape it in one or two additional movements. A technical aim should also be to avoid a bump in the inside concavity where the solid base becomes the wall

A good exercise is to see just how shallow a form can be made from a fairly vertical thinned wall.

During thinning the fingers are at right-angles to the curve being thrown at any given point. The left hand is usually higher than the right throughout the thinning and shaping of open forms. During the shaping process the inside hand may be relatively lower than in thinning.

Simply to demonstrate the difficulties of it, at some stage an attempt to narrow a thinned open form should be made.

Open forms do not necessarily have a wall of concave inside section. The wall may be straight or even convex. In throwing open forms every attempt should be made to explore as many possible types and variations of forms as possible. Though open forms are invariably turned a good technical aim is to throw them as evenly and thinly as possible.

44

Conical forms

Thrown forms in which the base is the widest dimension are probably the least commonly occurring of all forms used in pottery of the past.

Technically the movements used to make this type of form are very commonly used with other movements in the throwing of less simple forms. Isolating the movements is almost certainly of help to beginners.

85 The centred lump is initially spread out to a wide flat form

86 The small wall created by the opening action is bent inwards by the palms and is steadied by the fingers

87, 88 The position of the hands during upward thinning actions is the exact opposite of that used for open forms—the right hand exerts its pressure at a higher point than the left hand inside

85

86

88

87

89 During the second and third thinning movements as the left hand reaches down into the
bottom corner the top edge may be widened
and distorted. Providing it has not been over-
thinned it will not be difficult to control

90 Half way through the final thinning of the
wall an important action takes place which
enables forms to be thrown much narrower
than the width of a hand

Before actual collaring takes place the top edge
should be bent slightly inwards then the form
should be gripped by both the thumbs and the
index fingers at the point to which thinning has
been completed. The palms and fingers can if
necessary exert a slight downward inward
steadying pressure on the walls

91 The form is collared. The thumbs and fingers
push in on the wall moving upwards

92 After collaring the top of the form is thinned using one or two fingers only inside

93, 94 The form is thinned in three stages, the last complete thinning action is divided in two by collaring

95, 96 At the collared stage the section of the form is uneven. Shaping and thinning as a combined action begin just below the point where collaring was effective

This type is perhaps the most stable and adjustable in its plastic state of all thrown forms. The most likely point of collapse is the very base of the wall which if too thin tends to become eccentric during collaring. When still wide enough the form can be made wider and more convex with ease, even when too narrow the form can be adjusted from inside with the use of a long broad-ended rib. When narrow or enclosed the form can be narrowed at any point by pushing carefully inwards and moving the point of

97, 98 By using a second or third collaring action it should be possible to completely enclose this type of form. During closing it should neither become eccentric nor uneven in section

pressure upwards. Pushing gently either with the ball of the index finger or the side of the little finger of the right hand is the usual way of doing this.

A final shaping of some varieties of this form can lead to a very slight increase in height.

Though the form itself is rare it is one which is full of possibilities. The two techniques involved in throwing it—the inward throwing action and the collaring action—are very frequently used on more complex forms.

Waisted forms and spherical or ovoid forms

Throwing these two types of form is a combination of the techniques of the three forms so far described. If the processes of throwing the simpler forms have been mastered throwing either of these slightly more complex types of form should present no real difficulties.

Waisted forms

99 Centring and opening out is similar to that done with conical forms. The initial wall is bent inwards between the fingers and palm of the left hand assisted by the fingers of the right hand

100 Initial thinning is in an inward direction in the lower part and a vertical direction in the upper

101, 102 The second thinning establishes the inward and outward movement of the form. In the lower half the right hand is higher than the left as the form is thinned upwards and inwards. In the waist of the form the left hand moves upwards relatively more quickly and in the upper part of the form the left hand is slightly higher than the right as the form is thinned upwards and outwards

49

103 In its final thinning the form will be at its tallest. The sequence of final thinning and shaping will vary depending largely on the narrowness of the waist

104 The control with which final shaping can be done depends very much on the evenness of the thinning and on the consistency of the clay. If the waist or lower part of the form are too thin or if the clay is too soft, unevenness may easily be caused by the pressure, slight as it is, of shaping the upper part of the form

105, 106 During thinning the height of the form, and if intended, the width of the top should both show a steady controlled growth. It should be possible to keep the width of the waist constant at the minimum possible which allows the left hand to reach the bottom of the inside wall—but this will obviously not always be wanted. The procedure for making this type of form depends largely on the width of the waist. On forms where the intended width of the waist is sufficiently wide to allow the hand to reach the bottom, as illustrated, the whole form should be thinned and shaped in fairly complete actions

On forms where the intended width of the waist is too narrow to allow the left hand to reach the bottom, the lower part of the form should be thinned, collared and shaped to its final form (in the same technique as for conical forms) before the upper part of the form has been finally thinned and shaped. This, because of the collaring process, will result in a very different progression of forms from that illustrated. In this type of form it is important that the lower form and the waist have no weaknesses of excessive softness or thinness as these will make the thinning and shaping of the upper form difficult or impossible.

The shaping action described in the making of conical forms of pushing gently on the outside of the form only can be applied on the lower half of waisted forms but only with great care and only to a much more limited extent than with simple conical forms. Any suddenness or excess in this action puts the stability of the whole form above the waist in danger.

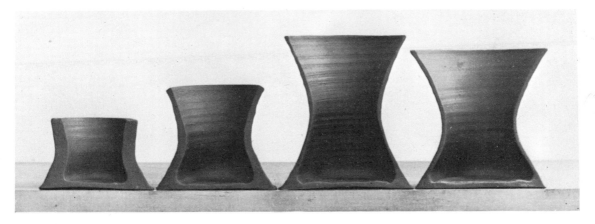

Spherical or ovoid forms

A good technical aim for beginners is to throw forms as nearly round as possible from a fairly narrow base and with a top diameter which just allows the left hand access to the inside wall.

107 The convexity of this type of form is created in the very first thinning movement

108 The second thinning movement increases the maximum width of the form

109 The final thinning action, which should rise as evenly as that on a cylinder and should create a wall of even thickness, creates the limits within which shaping can be done

110, 111 The relative position of the hands during both thinning and shaping corresponds in the lower part of the form with the position for open forms, the outside hand being lower than the inside, and correspond in the upper part of the form with the position for conical forms, the outside hand being above the inside hand

112, 113 The usual progression of this type of form is to increase in both height and width during thinning and, to increase in width losing some height during shaping

It should be perfectly possible to throw this type of form without any change in the diameter of the top from the first thinning to the final shaping.

It is often possible to complete this type of form without any shaping actions but finer control of form is possible if subsequent shaping actions are used.

Beginners should probably always use subsequent shaping actions whether a form is thought to be satisfactory or not as in doing this the limits to which any thinned form can be shaped are learnt.

Some narrowing of this type of form is possible in the inward curving top section of the form but is virtually impossible in the widest and lower sections.

The relative positions of the hands in throwing different forms may be clarified by these sectional photographs.

114 The point at which pressure is exerted by the inside hand is above that of the outside hand. This is the basic position for open forms, for the upper sections of waisted forms and for the lower sections of spherical forms

115 The points at which pressure is exerted on the inside and the outside are virtually level. This is the basic position for the widest parts of spherical forms and for the narrowest part of waisted forms. With spherical and waisted forms a truly horizontal position will exist for only an instant if the curves are of a continuous nature. With cylinders the hands will rise with the pressure between them exerted in a constantly horizontal plane

116 The point at which pressure is exerted by the inside hand is below that exerted by the outside hand. This is the basic position for conical forms, the lower parts of waisted forms and the upper part of spherical forms.

It should be noticed that the position of the right hand working outside changes much more than that of the inside hand

The way pressure is applied, whether it is through different fingers or through throwing ribs, does not alter the principles shown in these photographs.

Obviously the relative position of the two hands determines only the basic nature of the forms being thrown. The actual nature of forms is determined by the relationships of the pressure exerted by the inside and outside hands and by the direction in which the hands rise in space. In the widening parts of forms the inside hand usually exerts slightly more pressure than the outside. Narrowing parts of forms are less limited in the way they can be altered and pressure may be greater from either the inside or the outside hands depending on the intentions of the thrower.

Two points of great importance and of relevance throughout the throwing process, have not so far been mentioned, largely because they are so variable personally. The first is the speed of rotation at which throwing is done and the second is the amount of water used during throwing.

One of the first experiments a thrower should make, and by its nature it will be a gradual experiment, is to determine the speeds most suitable to different stages of throwing. Individual practice varies so much that only basic facts and a flexible rule can be stated. The facts that should influence the changes of speed are that the greater the speed of rotation the greater is the centrifugal force exerted on the clay; the thinner and softer the clay wall the greater is the effect of the centrifugal force; the wider the clay wall the greater is the centrifugal force at any given speed. The centrifugal force of rotation should at no stage be such that it affects control of any form during thinning or shaping. Centrifugal force is always present during rotation, when it is noticeable the speed of rotation is too great.

That the surface of clay should be lubricated with water throughout the throwing process has already been stated. How much water this involves will vary with the clay, the form being thrown and the individual. Two rules can be stated. Water should not be used to excess on the surface of a form. If water gathers in a pool in the base of a form it should immediately be removed with a sponge.

Learning many techniques is expensive in terms of material. Throwing is a happy exception to this as clay can be constantly re-used. Someone who is learning to throw should use this advantage to the full. Technical skill can only be fully developed through practice. Throwers should take every opportunity to practice and should make this practice as logical as possible.

All the basic forms described are capable of great variety and of subtle variety. By combining the processes of the basic forms virtually any possible form can be thrown. Fully exploring the possibilities of the technique should be the aim of the student thrower. In doing this, as well as constantly trying new and different forms, forms should be tried in very differing sizes—throwing a given form on a different scale may eliminate some problems and will probably create new problems.

It is very important that, when practising, throwers use differing clays—the best clay for throwing will often not be the clay most suitable for the finished nature of a given object.

In learning to throw considerable insistence should be placed on the thinness with which forms are thrown and on the amount of shaping which follows thinning. In fact during learning it is often a good idea to extend many forms until they collapse. An early insistence on thinness and on shaping should not be allowed to create a false picture for one of the qualities of throwing is that throughout the process forms are being made and changed. It is perfectly valid at any point during the throwing process for a thrower to decide that an object is finished—thinness and lightness are not necessarily qualities of forms made on the wheel nor are separate shaping actions a necessary part of the process of throwing. But technical accomplishment is incomplete if thinness cannot be achieved or if a thin form cannot be shaped to new forms.

The objects photographed in this section are simply thrown, they are not turned, neither are they trimmed of surplus clay. While initially the concern of the thrower will be simply with throwing and studying briefly the sections of the thrown forms before the clay is reprepared, some forms should be kept so that subsequent processes such as turning can be simultaneously learned.

When larger shapes of fairly full form are thrown some degree of taper in the wall is to be expected. Learning how thickly to throw certain forms in different clays is all part of the process of learning. The thicker parts of tapered walls are usually turned down. The more vertical a form the less of a taper should be necessary.

The beginner is well advised to expect many forms to collapse completely while throwing is being learned. Whenever a form collapses it should not, in haste or annoyance be immediately put on one side to be re-kneaded but should be cut in half with a wire to see if the reason for its collapse is inherent in the section of the wall.

Badly prepared clay usually makes itself obvious from the earliest stages of throwing and signs that the clay needs further preparation should be quickly learned by the beginner.

The reason for the collapse of most thrown forms can be seen from a section of the wall and it is usually due either to a wall being thrown too thinly or to a certain part of a wall being too thin for the form being thrown. Thinness alone is almost irrelevant and should always be gauged with the softness of the clay, the nature of the clay, the nature of the form being thrown and the size of the form.

Structural collapse due to thinness is easily recognised and understood. Some other types of fault are perhaps less obvious.

(a) Forms sometimes suddenly collapse opening up apparently inexplicably in horizontal and vertical cracks. When forms collapse in this way all forms develop a circular crack inside around their base.

117 Spherical forms usually in addition develop horizontal cracks at their widest point and vertical cracks at their widest point and the top edge.

118 Open forms in addition develop vertical cracks at their edge and usually other horizontal cracks.

This fault can be put down to any combination of a number of factors. Soft clay is more quickly prone to this cracking than firmer clay but the main reasons are rather to do with the thrower than the clay. An excessively long time spent working on a thinned form makes it increasingly more prone to this type of collapse. Allowing a pool of water to accumulate in the base of a pot and using excessive water on the walls of a pot makes this type of collapse an eventual certainty. In fact, if soft clay is thrown with excessive water for an excessive time this is bound to happen if it is not preceded by a more normal slumping collapse.

(b) Cracking of a different nature sometimes occurs near the top of open forms and the wider spherical forms (and can occur in almost all forms).

119 Whereas the previously described cracking is of a sharp linear nature this cracking is less clearly defined though it also is usually of a broadly vertical nature.

This fault is partly a fault in the clay and partly a fault in technique. When hard clay and soft clay have been mixed either by hand or in a pug mill the resultant mixture is often liable to this fault. It appears to be caused by incomplete mixing. Storing the clay removes the tendency to do this. The tendency is increased if thrown forms are stretched into more extended shapes by too much pressure from within rather than being thrown out-wards under more even pressure. This type of cracking can develop into the previous type if throwing is prolonged.

Clays which develop both these faults are referred to as 'tired' and should be well kneaded and stored for a few days

(c) A third, not uncommon fault but of a very different nature is a spiral buckling which sometimes occurs, usually in tall narrow forms.

120 The spiral eccentricities usually occur at the bottom of a form while the top is being worked. If the clay is not too soft and a cut section reveals that the wall is not unduly thin where the fault is then the fault can be put down to one cause with two possible reasons

The cause is that in exerting pressure to thin the wall at the top the hands have a braking effect causing spiral folding. This may be due to thinning not being done gradually enough, the lower wall, though not thin, being unable to take the pressure required to reduce excessive thickness at the top of the form. Or, it may be due to the clay or the hands not being wet enough and through lack of lubri-cation, exerting excessive pressure.

The fault can usually be remedied by rethrowing the form. The fault should not occur if tall forms are thinned in more stages than shorter forms using plenty of water.

Section 7

Turning

Turning is the process of paring away clay from a hardened but not dry thrown form. It is not inevitably a part of the process of making clay forms on a wheel.

When used, turning creates a range of possibilities of form and surface quite different from those of throwing.

In throwing the ratio of base width to maximum width of any thrown form is limited; in turning the base width of a previously thrown object can be reduced as much as is wanted immediately creating a proportion of form impossible to throw on all but the most minute scale. Angularity and sharpness can be produced in a form more easily by turning. Turning also creates the possibility of finely detailed beadings, which cannot be produced finely with a template while throwing.

Turning inevitably alters the surface of a form. To what extent the surface is altered will depend largely on the clay and on the intention. Turning will often be done solely to make a certain type of surface.

Turned form is created and limited entirely by thrown form. With the exception of surface alteration to bowls and other open forms when the inside may be slightly turned turning is done only on the base and outside walls of thrown forms. When turning is to be done on a form considerable attention should be paid to its inside form while it is being thrown.

The process of turning

Turning is done when pots are leather-hard.

Clay is leather-hard when it is easy to mark with a finger-nail but is difficult to mark with a finger. Leather-hard is a broad stage and the actual point at which clay can be best turned can only be determined by experience and is governed by preference. The clay should certainly not be so soft that the object still bends and it should not be dry.

Drying to a leather-hard condition should be a controlled process. If a thrown form tapers considerably and is dried too quickly it will dry at the top and yet be still quite damp at its base. This should be avoided either by slower drying or by placing the form upside down either on its top edge or resting on or in a chuck which should usually even out drying.

It should be remembered that a cold draught is more drying than a warm still atmosphere. It is of the greatest importance that forms being turned are of an even consistency in a horizontal plane. A turning tool will obviously affect clay of different consistencies differently. Some unevenness of consistency from top to bottom of a form can easily, and almost always is, accommodated in turning. Lateral unevenness, not uncommon if forms are placed near radiators or heating pipes or in a draught, can be accommodated hardly at all.

121, 122 Clay of the right consistency will pare away easily in long strands. If the consistency is the same over the whole of the turned area a finer control of surface quality is possible

When a thrown form is the right consistency (or preferably long before then) the best way of securing it to the wheel should be considered. There is a wide range of possibilities for open forms but a very limited choice for more enclosed forms.

(a) The simplest method of all is to invert the form and to secure it to the bat with coils.

123, 124 After the form is in position the bat should be dampened with a sponge before the coil is attached. The coil should be of firm clay and should be placed right up to the edge of the form and thumbed onto the bat only. A small coil of firm clay will hold forms more firmly than a large coil.

If the object is held in position with one hand while the coils are pressed down there should be no danger of it being pushed off centre. The drawback of this method is that its application is limited only to objects with edges that are substantial enough not to be damaged by any part of the process. The method ceases to be applicable to open forms where the edge is not the widest point

(b) An alternative to the previous method also resting the bowl on the bat is to have the coil, a much larger one in this case, on the inside of the bowl.

125 A fairly thick coil is placed centrally on the dampened bat and is evenly flattened

126 Its edge is turned down to the inside width of the bowl form and the width is checked with calipers

127, 128 The form is located and secured solely by the coil inside it

This method too is limited to forms where the edge is not likely to suffer damage. Removal, unless bats are used is difficult as the form cannot be slid off as in the previous method. Forms where the top edge is not the widest point can with care be turned with this method but there is a definite limit to a safe height. When a number of objects have to be turned, if a large coil is used and the widest form turned first, the coil can simply be turned down progressively for the smaller forms.

(c) This method involves the use of a hollow clay chuck. Hollow chucks are simply thickly thrown walls of clay which may or may not have a base. Where a large amount of throwing is being done a variety of sizes of hollow chucks on which to turn open forms and in which to turn enclosed forms is very useful. Clay chucks can be kept for a considerable time if wrapped in polythene bags when not in use. When they become somewhat harder than the consistency at which forms are turned they should be discarded.

A chuck thrown at the same time as the form it will receive if thrown on a bat will probably still be safely stuck to it. But if bats are not being used or when an old chuck is being used it will need firmly sticking to the wheelhead or bat. Methods of doing this vary, but only in detail.

129 The base of the chuck is scored with a fine toothed tool such as a hacksaw blade

130 The base of the chuck is held in water for a few seconds and the bat is moistened with thin slip and water

131 The chuck is placed on the bat as centrally as possible and its location immediately checked. The sticking action begins very quickly, the chuck can only be moved easily for perhaps fifteen seconds. If it is not located correctly within this time it will need to be forced off and re-stuck. A chuck attached like this will remain attached for a considerable number of hours. Sponging the bat and the chuck where they meet helps to keep the two stuck together. The edge of a chuck should be turned to make it absolutely centred. For open forms the edge should be turned into a convex downward and outward sloping edge, for enclosed forms it should be downward and inward sloping. There is no need in either case for the edge to coincide exactly with the curve of the form—this in any case would be virtually impossible to do or to check

Whether for open or enclosed forms the best consistency for a chuck is slightly softer than the object being turned, this difference does help to reduce any likelihood of the turned form slipping. It is a sensible idea to lightly sponge the edge of a chuck occasionally but this should not be overdone or the chuck and the form being turned may stick together—it is surprising with what tenacity joins can be made when they are least intended. Forms remain on or in their chucks by gravity and friction alone.

132, 133 One of the advantages of this method for turning open forms is that there is no limit to size. Very wide bowls are simply turned on chucks high enough to lift them clear of the edge of the wheel tray. Edge forms can suffer no damage in this process.

The position in the bowl form where the chuck can best be located will vary with the form of the bowl and with the amount of turning needed. If the whole of the outside surface is to be turned the diameter of support should not be too near the middle or the pressure of turning near the edge may tend to move the bowl on its chuck. Where a bowl form has a general angle of 45 degrees or more support will not be very stable—the shallower parts of a bowl curve give safer support. Gauging the clay consistency ideal for this method of support during turning will take a little experience through trial and error—everyone at some stage turns a bowl in this method and lifts it off to find a neat impression of the chuck edge deeply pressed inside. Forms being turned can be removed and replaced with ease to check the thickness

134, 135 For enclosed forms the chuck should have a convex downward and inward sloping edge. The form should be supported fairly near its widest point for maximum stability. This is the best way of supporting all forms with narrow openings at the top

(d) *136, 137, 138* Identical in principle to the hollow chuck is the solid chuck. The only advantage of a solid chuck over a hollow chuck is that when a large number of forms of greatly differing diameters are being turned only the one chuck is necessary if the largest is turned first and the smallest last

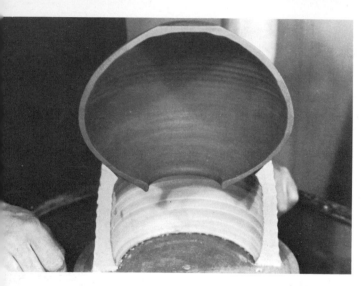

139

140

(e) One further way of turning enclosed forms is to refix them directly to the wheel. This process is limited in practice to forms where the lower part of the object is not at too sharp an angle to the wheelhead to be easily accessible. This process is more generally used before actual turning to remove some clay from large or especially thickly thrown form to facilitate even drying to the leather-hard stage than for actual finishing.

139 The base is roughed up and fixed to the bat in the identical way described for fixing chucks

140 Turning is done

141 If the top is sufficiently wide the thickness may be felt

142 The finished form will need a firm twisting action to remove it and the base can then be smoothed

(f) Cup chucks, made to locate jigger and jolly moulds, available for most bought wheels, can be adapted to form chucks for both open and enclosed forms

143 Cup chucks are available in several sizes and are located on the spindle of the wheel in exactly the same way as an ordinary wheelhead

141

142

144, 145 A firm even roll of clay is thumbed on to the dampened top edge

146 This can be directly turned down but it is perhaps easier and quicker to trim the top and edges with a wire. (See Section 8)

147 The top edge is turned to an approximate form depending on the object being turned

These are the main ways of securing forms to the wheel for turning. Variations on these methods are possible. A solid chuck is used by throwers engaged in producing large numbers of closely similar objects but the point of contact between the chuck and form is usually the edge of the form. Turning can be done in this way without stopping the wheel either to place, centre or remove the form but this requires practice and presumes edge forms not liable to damage.

143

145

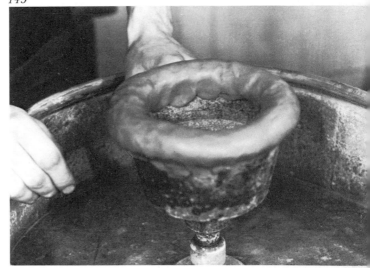

144

146

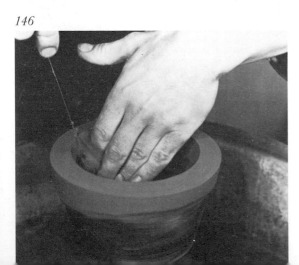

147

67

Centring forms prior to turning

The accuracy of the centring of any form being turned is of great importance. If an object is not well centred turning will make the walls on one side of a form thinner than the other and even if one side is not turned through the difference in thickness may easily be sufficient to cause warping or cracking or simply excessive fragility on the thin side.

It is inadvisable to attempt to turn forms which develop any eccentricity during throwing. Sometimes it is possible that some eccentricity is part of the quality of a form. When open forms develop eccentricity it is generally in the upper part of the walls of the form. Such forms can be turned safely and perfectly evenly if turning is restricted to the base and the lower part of the walls and if they are turned on a chuck which supports them on the centred base portion of the lower wall.

Open forms with slight eccentricity should be turned in method (c), (d), or (f). The care with which a thrown form is trimmed at the base has considerable bearing on the ease and accuracy with which it can be centred.

In method (a) open forms can be centred by locating them in concentric circles drawn on the wheelhead or bat with a pencil and with the wheel revolving or to the slight concentric grooves usual on machined metal wheelheads.

In method (b) an object is automatically located in the centre by the turned coil.

148 In methods (c), (d), (e), or (f), of support where the object being turned is simply placed on or in the chuck, the type of centring will vary with the type of form

149 Open forms like plates or dishes with a flat or very nearly flat inside surface when placed on a chuck will only show a horizontal swing when the wheel is revolving if they are not centred. Vertical unevenness will only be as much as is created by uneven cutting off. If such forms cannot be centred quickly by moving them slightly on the chuck a groove should be turned holding the hands very steady with a pointed tool near the edge of the base

150 When the wheel is stopped the difference between the trimmed edge of the base and this turned circle should be easily seen. In theory the form should be moved towards the point where the two circles are closest for half the distance in diameter between the two circles. In practice such mathematical precision is unnecessary for with experience the amount of movement necessary will be automatically gauged, indeed with experience the use of a turned circle will be unnecessary

151 When open forms of a continuous concavity or when enclosed convex forms are being turned respectively on or in chucks the form in theory will be centred when its base is in truly horizontal plane. If such forms are off centre unevenness at the base will be both horizontal and vertical. If difficulty is experienced centring such objects a firmly held pointed tool should be used to score marks lightly on the base. With the wheel stationary these marks will be seen to be either of a greater and a lesser depth, or of some depth and no depth, describing an incomplete circle. To be centred such objects have to be tilted downwards towards the point where the marks are of greatest depth. With open forms this involves moving them slightly across the wheel towards the point of greatest depth, with enclosed forms it involves tilting them in the chuck so the point where the marks are deepest moves downwards. With experience the making of such marks will probably become unnecessary

152 However experienced one is and (with the possible exception of method (b)) in whatever method the form being turned is supported it is a very good idea as soon as a form is centred to turn a circle lightly into the base to which the form can be re-centred should it move off centre or be removed from the wheel to check its thickness

153
154

155

153, 154 With experience both centring and re-centring can be done entirely visually or to the finger using the marking processes described only if unusual difficulty is encountered

In a technical sense only, turning is a much less exacting process than throwing. Leather-hard clay being obviously in a less impressionable state than soft plastic clay. Being a less exacting process the procedures of turning are more variable. Some general points are however of relevance.

The part of a thrown form most likely to have suffered damage in the form of indentations and other distortion in handling between throwing and turning is the edge of the base. Turning down an uneven surface is always more difficult than turning an even surface.

A good idea because it is probably quicker is to remove the edge of the base in one piece.

155 A deep groove is turned into the base an appropriate distance from the edge

156 Sometimes a further cut may be necessary inwards and upwards at the base of the wall. This will depend on the form and its thickness. Whether or not it is necessary the removed circle will come off complete

This process is by no means necessary but can save time and trouble.

Any form before it is turned or when it is removed from the wheel should be felt for its thickness and more important its inside form should be observed and clearly remembered.

157 Immediately the form is placed or replaced on the wheel one possibility while its inside form and its thicknesses are still clearly in the mind is to cut a number of concentric grooves of appropriate depth

158, 159 The form is then turned until the grooves are just removed

160 Whatever form is turned at the base of a form it is usually the last part of the turning process

156

157

158

159

160

One of a beginner's technical aims in turning should be to produce a form of constant thickness throughout. The described technique of making grooves and then turning them away can be profitably used two or three times removing the form from the wheel and checking between each action until the form is of equal thickness. Turning need not be a lengthy process. Once confidence is achieved the technique of turning grooves can be abandoned but it does give confidence while the technique of turning is new. A possible variation of the idea is to turn a long spiral groove and then turn it away repeating the process until it is thought sufficient clay has been removed. Cutting up thrown forms to study their sections is a common idea, cutting up turned forms is much less frequently done although just as much can be learnt from it. While being able to turn a form to an even thickness is an important part of learning to turn, many forms need to have walls which thicken towards the base if they are to be stable during firing. Technically learning to know the thickness of forms being turned is probably the most important aspect in learning to turn.

161, 162 Once confidence has been attained turning will be probably done without using any grooving process

163 A common convention with open forms is to turn a foot at the base. The function and origins of this are briefly discussed in Section 8. The form is made after all other turning has been done. This is probably because it is far easier to visually determine the possibilities of the height, width and form of a foot when the nature of the form it supports has been determined

164 When the outside form of the foot has been determined any concavity on its inside is turned out. This must be done only after the outside form has been determined or it can limit the foot to a greater width or lesser height than is wanted

165 Final attention is to smoothing the base of the foot which should have no roughness which could cause scratching when the form is fired and finished. Either a metal or a wooden tool held at a shallow angle to the surface quickly smoothes even the coarsest of clay pushing the grog into the clay. This smoothing is only possible if the clay has not been allowed to dry out too much

As has been said details of procedure may vary. A turning tool may be held still and turning done in a concentric way. Equally a tool can be moved slowly over the surface producing a spiral as in throwing—a downward movement creates the same spiral direction as does the upward movement of throwing, an upward movement creates the opposite spiral. Some amount of spiral ridging is created by most turning tools however closely and precisely they are used.

166 A broad edged tool such as a metal kidney can be used as a cutting tool and produces a hardly noticeable ridging. Held at a shallow angle to the surface, as here, it removes very little clay and has a smoothing polishing action. With fine clay extremely smooth surfaces can be turned with such tools.

167 Grogged clays provided they are not too hard can be smoothed in this way.

Speed of rotation during turning should not be too slow but varies considerably from person to person and should be varied to suit different forms and consistencies of clay. Differing speeds will produce different surfaces though the nature of the clay is an important factor in determining surface.

A tool can catch on serious unevennesses in a form in the early stages of turning and may drag the form off centre or right off the wheel. Any serious unevenness should be removed by scraping prior to turning. Uneven surfaces left by bad cutting off are best closely turned with a pointed tool which is less affected by bumps than a broad edged tool. The resulting finely ridged surface can be turned with a broad edged tool there being less body of clay to resist the tool.

Juddering is probably the only problem which may be encountered during turning. Juddering is when a turning tool bounces uncontrollably on a surface producing a radial ridging. It occurs most usually when broad edged tools are being used and is more frequent in coarse clays—often it can be started by an embedded lump of foreign matter which is why it frequently occurs in turning bodies with coarse grog. The remedy is to immediately turn the affected areas with a pointed tool and then remove the fine ridging. An alternative is to hold a kidney alternately at acute and obtuse angles to any radius—this pares clay off the raised edges of the radial ridging without sinking into and exaggerating the ridging which is what shorter edged turning tools tend to do. The best preventative is steadiness of hand.

Supports for the hands to rest on during turning similar to those fitted to lathes can be made but these should not be necessary. Steadiness of the hand is nevertheless of some importance. In most of the photographs in this section the left hand and the active right hand are touching each other. The left hand also simultaneously rests on the bowl surface. Where wide, open forms are being turned near their outside edge and are supported on hollow and solid chucks near their centre the left hand can be used to counterbalance the pressure of turning by pressing lightly on the opposite side of the bowl near the point of contact between bowl and chuck.

Neither throwing nor turning are difficult techniques but because turning is technically the more straightforward of the two much less space is devoted to it in the remainder of this book.

Technically only three things can go wrong irretrievably in turning. A form may be turned too thinly on one side either through eccentric throwing or bad centring.

It may be turned right through at any diameter through an incorrect gauging of its thickness. It may fly off the wheel through rough handling or inadequate support and excessive speed of rotation. None of these accidents should be difficult to overcome with practice; all are accidents due to inexperience rather than basic faults in turning technique.

Section 8

1 Cutting off

When the throwing of a clay form is complete it is removed from the wheel. Whether the form was thrown on a bat or thrown directly on the wheelhead a wire should be passed under it to release it. If forms thrown on bats are lifted off the wheel without being cut off there is a strong possibility that, as the clay hardens and begins to shrink a crack will develop across the base. (This crack may sometimes not occur until a form is dry or even fired but is caused by tensions set up at this early stage.)

Where a thrown form is not going to be turned the care with which it is cut off is of obvious importance but equal care should be exercised when a form is going to be turned for a level even base facilitates both centring for and the process of turning.

As has been mentioned in the section dealing with opening up a centred mass of clay a wire rises up slightly as it is passed underneath the base of a thrown form. This rising up is minimised if the wire is held tautly between the hands and is pressed down against the surface of the bat or wheelhead as it is passed under the thrown form.

Three methods are possible.

(a) *168* The wire is held tautly between the thumbs which press it down onto the bat. The wheel is stationary

169 The left hand remains stationary while the right hand moves towards the body, describing a rough circle around the pot

170 The left hand moves slightly towards the body and away from the centre of the wheel while the right hand moves round to near it. The wire emerges from the base of the pot in a horseshoe shape. In the latter stages the wire is taut only against the resistance of the clay not between the hands but is still held firmly down onto the wheelhead surface

(b) *171* The initial position of the hands is identical in this second method and the wheel is stationary

172, 173 The wire is kept taut between the hands throughout this process and the hands move simultaneously towards the body

(c) The last method is similar to the second but in this case the wheel is revolving slowly. This method requires the right hand to remain steady as it moves towards the body as it takes all the resistance of the clay as it rotates. Very little pulling pressure will be felt by the left hand. This process is often done as the wheel completes its last revolution before stopping. It should not be done with the wheel revolving fast or the released form may fly off the wheel.

There can be very little argument about the requirements of the base of a thrown form. It is the part of a form which will come into contact with all types of surfaces and it should not be likely to cause any type of scratching or denting damage. The base of any thrown form should be left as smooth as possible. When forms are left unturned the nature of the base will be determined to some extent at the cutting-off stage. The tool used to cut off forms is therefore of considerable importance.

When smooth clay is being used a single strand of brass wire or a strand of nylon or gut will give a smooth surface which should need no further attention except perhaps a light stroking with a rubber kidney. If the corner left between the cutting off and the trimming is too sharp it can be softened by lightly running the thumb or a rubber kidney round it when the clay is leather-hard.

With forms with wider bases or with coarse clays a single strand of wire may quickly break and a double strand of twisted brass wire is more usually used. A twisted wire can, of course, be used with smooth clays or narrow based forms.

The use of a twisted wire will result in a lightly grooved base. Where a twisted wire is used in the first or the third method of cutting off this grooving will take on a crescent form, which can with practice be controlled and varied.

If such markings are wanted they can be softened by a gentle stroking with the hands or a rubber kidney without any danger of eradicating them when this marking is combined with the use of a clay with coarse particles this softening process is necessary if the base is not to be too abrasive.

When the second method of cutting off is used the grooved markings will obviously be parallel. Grooved markings can be removed by firmly stroking the clay with a metal kidney. Where coarse clay has been used the base will always need attention with either a rubber or metal kidney to push protruding particles of grog into the clay.

When forms are lifted off the wheel on bats there is no need to use water during the cutting off process, but if the forms are to be lifted off by hand the wheelhead should be dampened just before the wire is used. The wire then drags some water through the cut which greatly facilitates lifting off.

When plaster bats have been used, cutting off is sometimes difficult. It is at the cutting-off stage that the correctness of the dampness of the plaster bat may be judged. If it is too damp the clay will not adhere to it and throwing will be difficult or impossible anyway. If a bat is too dry it will rapidly harden the base of a form making the lower sections difficult to throw and the cutting off difficult. The wire will tend to rise considerably in hard clay. A plaster bat used at the right degree of dampness will only slightly harden the base of a thrown form.

The second method of cutting off may tend to distort the base of forms thrown from less plastic clays, especially earthenware white clays and some porcelains, into distinctly oval forms. The first and third methods, which are identical in theory, exert a more or less equal pressure on the base at any given radius.

2 Lifting off

When throwing bats are not available forms will have to be lifted off the wheel by hand. Even if throwing bats are available it is as well to be able to do this. The two main procedures are easy and quick to learn.

(a) *174* The form has been cut off through water sponged onto the bat. The right hand begins to push gently but firmly on the trimmed base of the form. The left hand waits to receive it should it move suddenly

175 The form should slide easily across the bat. If it moves at all sliding will be easy. If it resists the pushing of the right hand it should be cut off again using more water. As it passes over the edge of the wheel the first finger of the left hand rests on the trimmed edge of the base while the other fingers and the palm move to support the base as it passes over the edge of the wheelhead

176 The form is then lifted onto a clean level surface and slid off the left hand the right hand being used to steady it and prevent it slipping.

The top edge of a form removed from the wheel in this way may distort from being round especially as it is slid off the hand. Providing it is cut off holding the wire conscientiously against the wheelhead and providing the surface onto which it is placed is flat the distortion of the edge should disappear when the form rests on the new surface. If the edge does not return to being round adjustments can be made by pushing on the base—experiments should be made on unwanted bowls to discover how much pressure in what direction on the base is necessary to make adjustments to the eccentricities of the top edge

(b) 177 Water does not necessarily have to have been used during cutting off for this method of removing forms. Both hands are cupped loosely around the lower part of the form. As a soft thinly thrown form can be easily dented pressure should be spread as much as possible using as much of the palms and fingers as possible in lifting the form. If a resistance to lifting is felt a slight twist or a slight sliding action may free the form. The little fingers of each hand should grip the form at its very base. More pressure can be exerted at the base as there are no thin walls liable to denting

178 The form is lifted gently on to a flat clean surface. The hands should be removed slowly so that if slightly stuck they do not distort the form

The first method is more suitable for open forms as tall forms can neither be lifted nor slid off safely from the palm of the hand. The second method is more suitable for enclosed forms. Open forms picked up in this manner would tend to simply fold up while with enclosed forms the folding is resisted by the upper part of the form. With reasonably rigid clay and some practice it should be possible to lift simple small and medium sized forms from the wheel with no danger of either denting or general distortion.

For both methods the hands should be cleaned of slip and clay. For the first method the left hand should not be dry or it may be difficult to slide the form from it. The second method is most easily learnt if the hands are dry, when they will tend to stick slightly to the surface of the form. As soon as some confidence has been achieved the method should be tried with the hands clean but wet.

While it is a good idea to learn both these lifting techniques for removing forms from the wheel it is far more convenient if bats can always be used. Some clays, especially white earthenware bodies and some porcelains, have not the rigidity to be lifted off the wheel with any degree of safety. Large forms, especially large open forms, whatever clay they are thrown in are extremely difficult to remove from the wheel except on bats.

In the first method only those parts which in any case will probably be turned are touched so the surface will not be affected by lifting off. In the second method, providing the surface is not excessively coated with slip and providing the hands are clean and wet marking of the surface will be minimal but cannot be entirely avoided. Forms where the surface quality, of whatever nature it is, is important and is considered as finished at the thrown stage should only be lifted off if there is no other alternative.

3 Trimming the top of a thrown form

A form, well thrown, from a well centred and opened out piece of well prepared clay should develop no unevenness either in the thickness of its wall or in its height.

A marked unevenness of thickness in the top edge (or in any other horizontal section) of a thrown wall of clay suggests the presence of clay of an uneven consistency. If the unevenness in

thickness is more than slight the form should probably be scrapped and the clay reprepared. If the unevenness is only slight it can sometimes by the application of firm but light pressure be changed into a vertical unevenness making the form of uneven height.

If the top edge of a form is of uneven height through some fault in centring, opening up, thinning or in clay preparation or if it is simply taller than is wanted the form can be cut down to a lower even height by one of several methods.

Any reasonably thin wooden or metal tool can be pushed through the revolving wall to the inside hand and the clay from the top lifted off. With practice, if the clay wall is still thick, clay can be removed using a finger or thumb to push through the wall to the hand on the inside. The most usual two methods use a needle set into a cork or a wire.

Trimming with a wire

179 The wire, either a single strand or a twisted double strand, is held taughtly between a finger of each hand. The left hand is over the inside of the form, the right hand is outside its edge. The wheel is revolving

180 The wire is lowered quickly a short distance into the wall of the form and is held briefly at a constant height

181 A looseness in the severed top section will be seen and felt after a very few revolutions. The hands still keeping the wire taught move forwards and upwards lifting the clay clear of the form. The rising action should not be too rushed or the wire will cut through the severed piece instead of removing it

Trimming with a needle or pin

182 The revolving wall is gripped lightly between the fingers and thumb of the left hand. The right hand holding the needle is steadied on the left thumb.

183 The needle is pushed through until it touches the fingers of the left hand.

184 The left hand then grips the clay slightly more firmly and both hands rise forwards and upwards

With both these two methods the speed of the revolution of the wheel is not very important but should not be too great. When the second method is being used the lifting action can be quicker than with the first method as the thin cutting tool does not do the lifting unaided. The importance of the needle in the lifting action can be demonstrated by attempting to lift off the clay with the left hand alone.

With both methods the amount of clay which can be removed at one time is limited. When a considerable height of clay is being removed or when even a small amount is to be removed from a very wide form it is a surer practice to remove the needle, simply by withdrawing it, or the wire, by giving it a sharp upward lift, to stop the wheel and to lift and peel off the clay with both hands. If this is not done in these cases there is some considerable risk that the removed clay will not clear the form and will land draped on its edge half inside, half outside at worst distorting the form and at least being awkward to remove.

In most instances, however, the two illustrated methods are efficient, but both leave a hard angular edge which if not wanted will have to be altered with the fingers.

185

186

187

4 Edges on thrown forms

The appearance of any form is considerably qualified by its details. Edge details play an important role in conditioning the appearance of any thrown form.

Edges clearly can be thick or thin, they can be simple or complex. It is only perhaps when an attempt has been made to throw identical edges that the infinite subtle variations possible are realised and appreciated.

Technically, the basic nature of an edge should be determined fairly early in the throwing of a form. An edge can be thickened up after all thinning and shaping of the rest of the form has been completed, it can also be thinned out at this stage. Both these actions can cause wobbling on small thinly thrown forms. It is the best practice to have a fairly clear idea of what sort of edge a form will have and to form it throughout the making of the form.

185, 188 After very little thinning has been done the general form of the edge is made

186, 189 Providing some care is exercised subsequent thinning action will not distort the edge and after each thinning action the edge form is steadied and perhaps adjusted slightly

187, 190 When all thinning has been done the edge can be finally formed

Edges can be formed by the fingers alone. They can be smoothed by holding a thin strip of fine chamois leather over them. This will remove slip which sometimes gathers at the top of forms.

191 The chamois leather should be held lightly between the hands and held gently round the edge. A chamois leather will have a far less deforming effect than a sponge and tends to push grog into the clay while a sponge pulls it out and cuts up the surface

188

189

191

190

Edges can also be formed by templates. Templates can be made out of various materials—wood, metal and fired clay being the most common. They are flat in form and should be bevelled towards their working edge. Templates give a clean, hard precise quality to an edge—their use in history has been greatest in periods when clay form was strongly influenced by metal forms. Being time consuming to file, the danger is that templates are over-used or are used out of context. Hardboard is a sensible material from which to file templates. It is easy and fairly quick to file and does not last too long.

192 The template has little or no cutting action and its use should not be rushed. It should first trail on the surface of the clay then be brought round to point to the centre then be removed. A single decisive action will give the cleanest results. Some slip and soft clay will gather on its back surface during the action and this should be wiped off the template should a second action be necessary. Throughout the action the left hand resists the inward pressure on the wall caused by the use of the template

To appreciate the variety and importance of edges it is an excellent idea to take a number of lumps of clay of equal weight and to throw closely similar forms all with differing edges. The heights of the forms will vary depending on the amount of clay used in the edges but this will detract little from studying the differences and their effects.

193–203

5 Trimming the base

During throwing it is impossible to use all the clay on the wheel. A small outward curving form of surplus clay is usually left at the base of the wall (this form can be seen in the profile photographs of forms in Section 6.) Were this form simply left it would be sharp and very liable to get chipped and broken. Basically there are two conventional ways of treating the bottom edge of a thrown wall when no turning is envisaged. Either more clay is left at the bottom than is naturally surplus and either with the fingers or tools is shaped into a protruding form or the natural surplus is trimmed off with a tool often giving the main form a slight undercut. When trimming is used it is often the last action before cutting the form off with a wire. It can, however, precede final thinning and shaping actions. Both alternatives are open to great variation, trimming being the more frequently used.

When trimming thrown forms with any throwing tool it must be realised that the wet clay reacts very differently to leather-hard clay, having very much less resistance to pressure. Almost all tools have as much pushing effect on the clay as they do cutting. For simply removing clay a long narrow pointed tool is best.

204 The tool is pushed into the clay along the line of its top edge. If the top edge of the tool is pushed against the wall by moving it in a line from its point to its middle a considerable and uneven ridge of clay is formed on the wall above the trimming. This can be removed with the finger but if the tool is used correctly it will not develop there being no pressure on to the wall from the top edge of the tool. The tool is pushed right down to the bat and is then withdrawn

205 The tool is pushed inwards again, its lower edge resting on the bat and the clay, already separated from the form but still revolving on the bat, is removed. When a considerable amount of clay is being removed this inward action may take more than one motion for if too much clay is allowed to gather on the tool it may push upward on to the trimmed form and stick to it

206 Further adjustments to the extent or the angle of the trimming can then be made. Concavity or convexity if wanted are made at this point by lightly pressing a tool of appropriate form against the clay

207, 208 It is arguable that the trimmed area as well as the flat base area should on all forms be non-abrasive. With smooth clays trimming should result in surfaces which need no further attention but with coarse clays trimming results in a very rough surface. Roughness can very easily be removed by simply holding a wooden tool at a shallow angle to the surface and lightly pressing. The tool can be straight edged or convex or concave depending entirely on intention

209 A final very small undercut is sometimes made to hide any unevenness made in the subsequent cutting off process. This is a good idea with both smooth and coarse clays when a crispness of forms has been part of the objective in throwing—the upper edge of the small secondary undercut can with care be unaffected by manual smoothing of the base

210 Templates can be used to make simple undercuts but their use is more typical where details which could be formed in no other way in soft clay, such as beadings, are wanted.

Templates are simply pressed lightly against the clay surface, the pressure is supported by the left hand inside the form. Clay is displaced into the form of the template by pressure. Very little clay should or need be removed. A template remains cleanly effective only while there is not too much clay on its back surface. The best action is to pivot the template slowly starting at a shallow angle to the surface, moving until at right angles then to take it off and clean it and if necessary repeat the action. It is a good idea to remove water and slip from the surface with a sponge or a throwing rib before using the template otherwise it quickly tends to become covered in slurry on its back surface

211, 212, 213

An instructive exercise is to throw a number of forms as closely similar as possible and to trim each one differently varying the extent of the angle and the concavity or convexity of the trimming. (See page 92.)

6 Turned feet

214–225 The convention of turning hollow feet into the base of forms is by no means limited to open forms but it has been far more commonly applied to them than to more enclosed forms

There seem to be three main reasons for the convention. If the glaze is cleaned off a foot-ring, some flowing movement of glaze during a firing can be safely tolerated before forms stick to the surfaces on which they are fired. For this reason foot-rings were used extensively in the Orient on forms glazed with high fired felspathic glazes. Such glazes always tend to move but rarely flow. Low fired earthenware glazes tend to run extensively if they move at all during firing and turned foot-rings cleaned of glaze are in fact found less extensively on earthenware of any date or provenance.

A universally applicable reason for foot-rings is that an open form of round inside form is rendered stable without being left heavy.

The third reason equally universally applicable is that forms raised up from the surface on which they stand are more easily seen and can be given a visual lightness. This, combined with safety of firing glazed forms, is probably of equal importance in explaining Oriental foot-rings. Visual lightness appears to have been the main reason for the development of foot-rings on the unglazed pottery of the Greeks. It should be said immediately and equally it should be obvious that the mere presence of a foot-ring does not necessarily remove the danger of a form sticking during firing or make it stable or make it visually light. If a glaze is over fired or too thickly applied no reasonable amount of foot-ring will be sufficient to prevent it sticking to the surface on which it rests during firing. The stability of a form depends on the depth of a form and its foot and the relationship of its width to the width of its foot. Visual lightness depends on the qualities of the form of the objects as well as their proportions.

Whatever the reasons for using or rejecting the convention of the foot-ring in any given instance no problems should be encountered in turning providing the throwing has left sufficient clay for the required form. Foot-rings are enormously variable forms both generally and in any specific instance—the nature of turning is only fixed within fairly broad limits by throwing.

A good exercise is to throw a number of closely similar bowls and to see how differently they can be turned within the limits created by the throwing and to study the different visual effects of the forms and proportions.

7 The use of throwing ribs

Throwing ribs are not templates and are used in a quite different way. While a template moves only slightly in a horizontal plane when in use a throwing rib is moved over the whole surface rising vertically. The function of a template is to make a form, often a detail, the primary function of a throwing rib is to remove slip from the clay surface and in doing so to smooth the surface. Considerable shaping can, however, be done with throwing ribs and with fuller forms it is an easier practice to use the ribs initially on a fairly vertical form and then to open it out rather than attempting to smooth an already full form.

Ribs can be used on outside forms only, inside forms only or both inside and outside. When used on one surface only a hand must support the pressure on the opposite surface.

While the most usual function of ribs is to smooth, and to finally shape smoothed forms, ribs are sometimes used in the thinning of forms.

When ribs are used no further water need be used on the clay surface, the dampness of the clay itself being sufficient to prevent excessive friction between the rib and the clay which might cause the lower part of a form to flap in the manner of fault (c), in Section 6. It might seem in theory as the clay is not being dampened when ribs are used that more extreme forms might be possible. In practice this is rarely so, unsteadiness of hand or faulty technique being more often responsible for collapsing than the softness of clay.

A slight concavity in the edge of a rib is sufficient to enable it to be used on almost any convex surface. Ideally a variety of ribs is more convenient. For thinning a slightly convex edged rib is best.

226 Ribs are held between the thumb and fingers and at a fairly steep angle to the surface. They move over the surface in the same steady rising action as the hands

227 A metal kidney may be used in much the same way as a rib. Being less rounded it should be held at a shallower angle to the surface than a rib

In the first upward movement a rib of any type should be tilted forward with the rotation of the wheel at its top end. In this position slip from the surface of the form tends to gather on its back surface rather than being left on the surface in a spiral ridge. The rib should be cleaned when a large amount of slip has gathered on its back surface. The form can be sponged before a rib is used to minimise the build-up of slip.

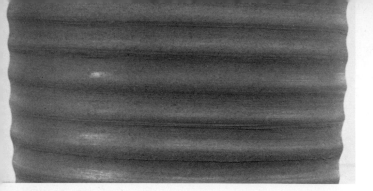

8 Surface

The clay from which the form is made, the temperature of firing and whether the firing is oxidising or reducing and the use of slip, glaze and of graphic ornament are all factors which can be of great importance in qualifying the nature of a final surface. Of prime importance, however, in determining the nature of the final surface is the quality of surface formed at the throwing or turning stages. Once the thrown or turned surface has been made while there are still many possibilities open and while the thrown or turned surface may not be the most obvious quality of the final surface something basic in the final nature of the surface has been determined.

It is an idea for all beginners at some stage to devote time to the intentional creation of differing surfaces. One interesting way of doing this is to differ only the surfaces of otherwise closely similar forms. A possibility that should not be overlooked is the possible gradation of the nature of surface of a single form. Interesting possibilities exist in the combination of turned and thrown surfaces on a single form.

Intention, the clay used and tools are the three most important factors in determining the nature of surface in both throwing and turning.

Thrown surface

228–233 In both thinning and shaping clay forms with the hands some slight degree of spiral ridging is inevitable. The spacing of this ridging can be varied by varying the speed of the wheel and by varying the rate at which the hands rise. The depth of the ridging can be increased by decreasing the area of pressure during thinning and shaping and can be decreased by increasing the area of pressure. If the end of the index finger alone is used ridging will be much deeper than if the whole of the side of it is used. Ridging can be virtually eliminated by the final use of sponges or chamois leather or by the use of a metal kidney or wooden ribs. Smoothness produced by metal or wooden tools at the throwing stage is obviously different to the smoothness possible with the hands alone but is also different to the varieties of smoothness possible during turning.

Whether a clay is grogged or not has less

effect on thrown surface than might be imagined.

If the hands alone are used grog is a limiting factor on the nature of the edge but has little textural effect on the surface. If sponges, especially synthetic ones, are used on the surface the grog does immediately become noticeable as it becomes lodged in the sponge surface and tends to cut up the surface of the form in fine lines. Chamois leather has this cutting up effect to a much lesser extent. Metal and wooden smoothing tools tend to quickly push the grog into the clay forming surfaces punctuated by short lines scored by the grog before it is pushed into the clay. Of perhaps greater effect than either grog or sand in a clay is the speed with which the clay forms slip from the water used during throwing. This obviously will vary with the amount of water a thrower uses but does certainly vary greatly from clay to clay. So much slip is formed in some cases that even when the clay surface is smooth the slip on its surface forms noticeable ridges. On surfaces ridged by the fingers the slip tends to hang on the under side of the ridges. This slip can, if so decided, be removed by sponge or wooden or metal tools and the cleaned surface then again worked on by hand.

By logical experiment with differing clays each individual will evolve ways of forming and controlling thrown surface.

Turned surface

234–239 Being a non-lubricated cutting process, as opposed to the lubricated squeezing process of throwing, and as the clay is in a considerably firmer condition the nature of clay is of greater effect in turning. The textural nature of the clay is revealed as soon as clay is removed. The exact nature of the surface created during turning whether clay is smooth, sandy or heavily grogged varies considerably with its degree of dryness. As explained in Section 7, it is possible, unless a clay is too dry, to smooth even the groggiest of clays.

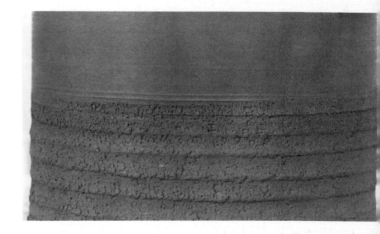

The depth of ridging produced during turning depends on the shape of the tool and the pressure applied to it. The spacing of ridging depends on the speed of revolution of the wheel and the speed of movement of the hands.

If the left hand rests on the clay during turning either to steady the form or to steady the right hand it has, often, a noticeable softening effect on turned ridges and on the granular textures which result from the turning of grogged and sandy bodies.

It is perhaps easier to vary the surfaces of a single form in turning than it is in throwing.

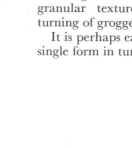

9 Tools

While actual throwing can be done with virtually no tools at all, a number of tools are of possible use. Many tools can be used—any choice is largely one of preference.

Sponges A selection of both natural and synthetic should be available.

A sponge on a wire or stick is useful for getting water out of the bottom of forms with narrow tops.

240

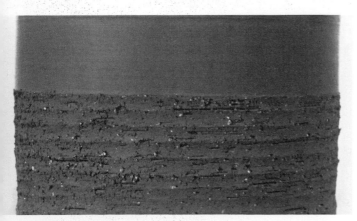

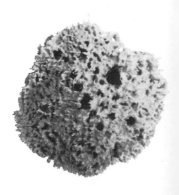

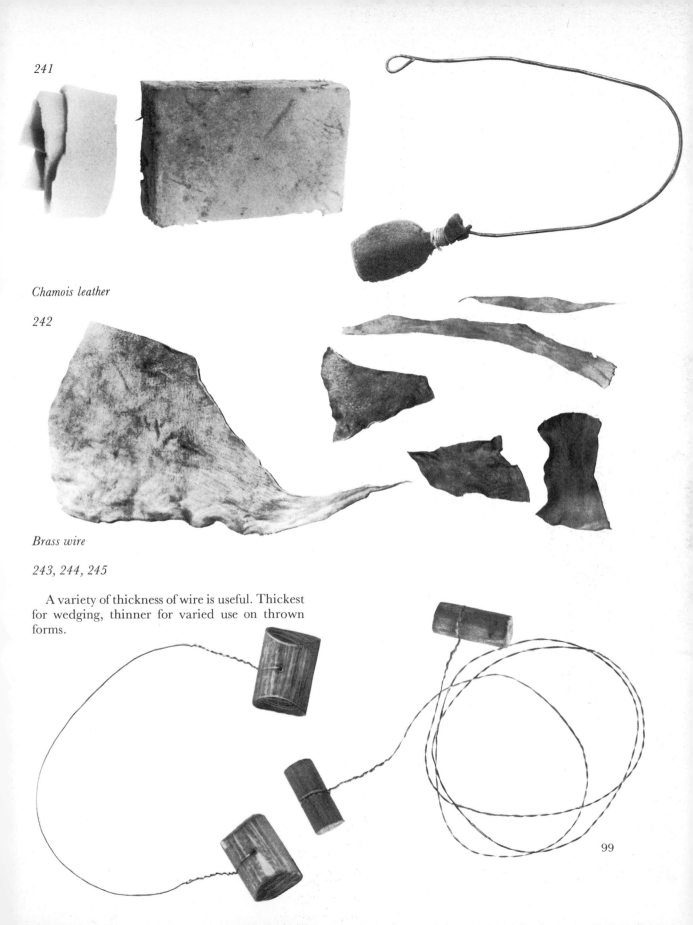

241

Chamois leather

242

Brass wire

243, 244, 245

A variety of thickness of wire is useful. Thickest for wedging, thinner for varied use on thrown forms.

99

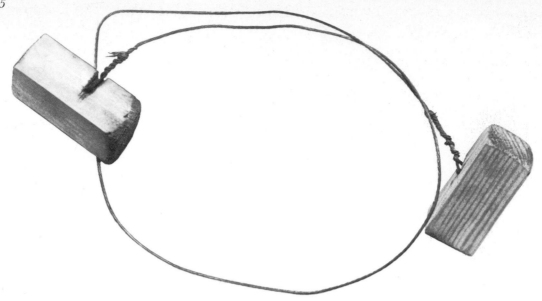

Turning tools A variety of shapes in stainless steel or iron—for obvious reasons these should never be sharpened where the filings will get into the clay.

246

Turning tools Bent packing case wire bound with string and wire modelling tools are sometimes useful as turning tools.

247

Wooden modelling tools   Of use during trimming.

248

Calipers with brass wing nut and bolt, are better than those with steel as the steel is quickly rusted by damp clay. If fitted with the correct washers they can be tightened so they are moveable but do not slip when set.

249

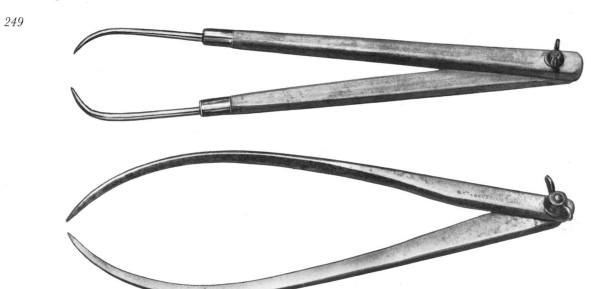

Needles should be firmly set into cork.
    A knitting needle is a possible substitute.

250

Palette knives and old rulers are useful in removing small forms thrown on a clay lump.

251

Throwing ribs are durable if made from hard wood but wear quickly if made in soft wood. Wear can be minimised by a good beeswax polish.

252

Templates can be filed in hardboard but if considerable use is planned, copper is preferable.

253

Rubber kidneys are useful for smoothing the bases of pots. They can be bought with differing rigidities.

254

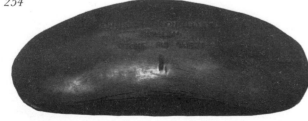

Metal kidneys can be used as throwing ribs but are more frequently used, as are hacksaw blades, on the bases of forms.

255

10 'Throwing and turning'

The term 'thrown and turned' is a specific term descriptive of an industrial technique. The entire noticeable surface of objects made in this technique is turned—thus open forms are turned over their whole surface inside and out; more enclosed forms are turned over their whole outside surface the inside usually being formed or at least smoothed with a rib at the throwing stage.

The process is now used to only a slight extent in the industry. Both the throwing and the turning are done very quickly and at high speeds of rotation. Objects in their thrown state look heavy and indefinite and are in fact fairly thickly thrown but are even and extremely precise. Turning is invariably not done by the thrower and is usually done on a horizontal lathe. Such is the precision of throwing that a turner, even when turning narrow-topped objects never bothers to look at the inside thrown form.

The technique arose for probably three main reasons. Before moulding and casting were extensively used it was the best way of producing forms with the very smooth surfaces necessary for some types of graphic decoration. The early frit porcelains of Europe were too non-plastic to be thrown into thinly potted forms and 'throwing and turning' was a way of forming such synthetic bodies into shapes of acceptable lightness. Probably the most important reason and certainly the reason why the technique is still used is that forms of great complexity or more often fairly simple forms with complex details such as bead-ings can be more quickly and surely made than by moulding—in fact some thrown and turned objects would be virtually impossible to mould and cast.

If industrial thrown and turned forms are examined some reason will usually be found why they were not slip cast or jigger and jollied.

'Throwing and turning' was slightly used by almost all cultures at some time but its most famous manifestation is the work done in England and Western Europe in the eighteenth century. The aesthetics of this work, except where graphic ornament was applied, revolved around the qualities, proportions and forms of the smoothed surfaces and around the placing and forms, often very elaborate, of the turned bead-ings. The influence of contemporary silverware was very strong.

Turning of almost any type is as easy on a wheel as on a horizontal lathe.

One of the reasons for turning given in Section 7 is for the alteration of surfaces. This in fact is really all that 'throwing and turning' is.

The importance of beadings, of smoothness and of the style of the eighteenth century are simple conventions of the technique. They are not an essential part of it.

Except when very non-plastic bodies are used 'throwing and turning' is only a conventionally separate process rather than a technically different one from throwing and then turning. Whenever turning is done one of the aims should be to freely exploit those surfaces and forms and details that it makes possible.

11 Repetition

It is as fallacious to think that forms repeated in quantity are lacking necessarily in quality as it is to think that a unique form is of necessity endowed with quality.

Many people when learning to throw view with complete antipathy the idea of trying to throw two or more identical forms. There are, nevertheless, some lessons to be learnt and advantages gained from exercises in repetition throwing.

The usual procedure for repetition throwing is to have the prototype form on the ledge of the wheel to use calipers for width, a ruler, perhaps, for height and weighed pieces of clay and the usual aim is to make many identical forms.

This, at some stage, is a worthwhile exercise.

One thing it does bring home is that the realisation of most forms differs greatly from their conception.

With such exercises the results are all too often tired, overworked forms. Perhaps a better insistence in initial exercises than one on similarity is an insistence on speed.

It is a good idea to set ones own time limit and to stop work on each form when the time limit has expired. This at least stops forms from being over worked. All the forms should be kept and when all the prepared clay has been used they can be compared. Even though the aim has been to make closely similar forms the results will almost certainly differ considerably. If the thrower is more experienced they may only differ slightly. Where the eventual aim is not standardised production of forms, the most important part of repetition throwing is in studying the subtle and the more obvious differences which result. If the aim has been to throw forms quickly (not too quickly, but certainly not too slowly) the results of most beginners, and more experienced throwers' essays in repetition are usually far more successful as exercises in variation. This does not matter at all but that it is appreciated is of the utmost importance.

Making fifty forms the same may, in that it is a repeated and learnable rhythm, increase the confidence of beginners but it cannot increase their depth of knowledge of technique as only one problem is faced rather than the many which would be faced if fifty different forms were thrown.

Any process arguably loses its validity, except for the lazy minded, if it creates a state of boredom. And if this is the effect of repetition it is better stopped than laboured.

Perhaps more broadly instructive processes, such as exercises in variation and progression, are better, certainly they are a complement to exercises in repetition. Twenty forms between a cylinder and a sphere; twenty forms between a sphere and a hemisphere; forms of identical profile and differing widths; forms of identical widths and differing heights; complex combinations of forms. The possibilities are endless and each person should invent and set his own exercises.

Initial exercises should be towards increasing technical ability but also towards developing an appreciation of the possibilities and subtleties of form.

12 Throwing ridges

Ridges can be applied as coils to leather-hard forms and thrown to a final even shape. They can equally be incorporated during the throwing of a form. The procedure is simple but does differ from throwing actions so far described.

256 Thinning begins normally but halts below the first ridge

257 Thinning begins again a small distance above where it ceased leaving as much clay as is wanted. Thinning continues to the bottom of the next ridge

258, 259 Thinning resumes above the next ridge and continues to the top. This procedure is repeated for as many ridges as are wanted

260 The ridges are thinned outwards by squeezing between two fingers or between thumb and first finger of the right hand. After they have all been thinned as much as is wanted a further final thinning of the walls of the form can take place

261 Within limits further shaping of the form should be easily possible

Though the technique is perhaps of limited application making forms in this way is an excellent exercise in the control of thickness and thinness in thrown walls.

One technical aim in making this type of form should be to avoid concavities in the inside form corresponding with the ridges outside as these lead quickly to instability. This can best be avoided by using the side of the left hand index finger on the inside during the initial formation of the edge and also during any thinning of the ridges (*260*). While the ridges are thinned a slight inward pressure of the two fingers outside should be combined with their squeezing action. This must not be so great as to thin the walls too much but it will help to prevent the inside form being affected by the outward movement of the clay of the ridges. Shaping the fairly vertical thinned form to a fuller shape is an excellent exercise in developing control for throwing less complex forms. The technical aim should be to make the walls of the form evenly and hardly different in thickness to the walls of an unridged form of comparable scale.

Visually the placing of the ridges on a form and the distances between them are obviously of as much importance as the nature and extent of the ridges themselves. As the clay from which the ridges are formed has to be left in the wall before final thinning and shaping, judging the amount of clay that will form a certain ridge and the initial spacing that will result in a certain final spacing is a matter of experience.

13 The use of calipers

When the intention of throwing is to produce two or more closely similar forms calipers are a useful measuring tool. After an initial form has been thrown, they are opened out and adjusted until they record the width at a given point, often the width of the top of the form. The width of the same part of the second form is then checked against the calipers and any necessary adjustments are made. Adjustments to increase the width are nearly always easier than to narrow it. The actual use of calipers in this process requires no special procedure.

It will often, however, be necessary to convert an inside measurement into an outside measurement as for example when a lid is being made or when a bowl is being secured for turning by the method described on page 60 (method (b)). This requires a more definite procedure if accuracy is to be achieved.

Caliper arms are almost always curved. When the two points of the arms touch an arch shape is formed between the arms. When an inside diameter is being measured the arms are crossed by pushing them together and then, if the distance is great, by pulling them further apart for the necessary amount. When an outside measurement is being taken the arms are simply pulled apart until the points describe the required distance. In the first position measuring an outside diameter or in the second position measuring an inside diameter by holding the calipers above the form and guessing is extremely unreliable.

262 Where two pairs of calipers are available measurements can be converted easily and quickly by simply adjusting a second pair until, in the opposite position its points coincide with those of the first pair.

When only one pair of calipers is available this transference of measurements is equally easy but slightly slower

263 The inside diameter of a top edge is recorded

264 This measurement is transferred carefully in pencil on to any available surface. Two knife marks on a lump of soft clay are equally accurate

265 The calipers are then opened out to these marks

266 With the calipers in their new position the measurement of the other form is checked

In transferring outside measurements to inside the procedure is, obviously, exactly reversed.

14 Lids

While describing the making of specific functional articles is not within the scope of this book a brief description of some of the many techniques in which lids can be made is not inappropriate.

Lids either have a locating seating embodied in their own edge or fit into a seating in the edge of the form they cover.

267 A lid with a seating in its own edge

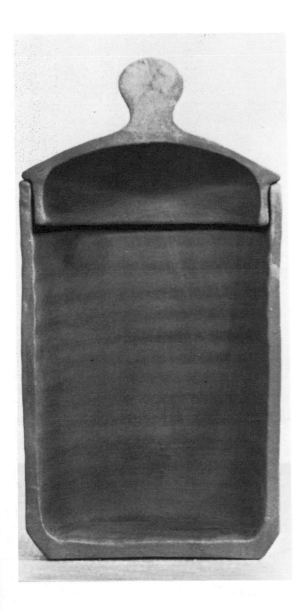

268, 269 Lids located in a seating on a main form

270, 271 Lids which both have seatings in their own edge and are located in the seating on the edge of the main form are usually found on vessels designed to contain and pour liquids. The theory is that if during pouring the lid begins to tip its vertical flange will impinge on the horizontal flange of the pot preventing it from falling out. If the tolerance in the fitting is kept to a minimum the vertical flange of the lid does not need to be very deep.
Lid seatings are only specific edge forms

Throwing a lid seating

272 A fairly broad flat edge is made in the first thinning. Before all thinning is complete this is bisected by holding the edge underneath with the thumb and a finger of the left hand and pushing down halfway across the edge with the end of the first finger of the right hand. The edge form should be begun but not finished at an early stage

273 Subsequent thinning and shaping without distorting the edge is perfectly possible

274 The final action should be to rethrow the seating more precisely, the flat part should be horizontal and there should be a distinct angle where the vertical edge starts

Edge seatings on lids and pots should not be too thin otherwise they will damage easily. The edge should be substantial enough to be smoothed with a chamois leather, if so wanted.

Lids, depending on their form and on their seating, are thrown either upside down or the right way up.

Some flat lids can be thrown the right way up.

275 The centred mass of clay is spread out leaving clay for the knob

276 When the knob is formed a vertical wall is thrown at the edge and is trimmed. Its width should correspond with the inside width of the form it will cover

277, 278, 279 The top edge of this wall is bent over outwards until it is horizontal taking especial care to keep the lower part of the wall vertical and not to alter its width.

Flat lids designed to fit into the seating on a pot may be made this way but without the necessity of the edge form

Domed lids, deep or shallow, may be made the right way up by the collaring process described for conical forms in Section 6.

As with all collaring processes the top edge must at no point be allowed to get too thin.

280, 281, 282 The accurate width of the vertical flange is fixed at this stage. Throwing from this point on is only from above the horizontal and vertical flanges

Slight shaping of the enclosed form is possible, as with all conical forms, by exerting a slight inward pressure on the thinned walls.

The only turning which should be necessary is on the inside of the flange which has to be left fairly thick to take the weight and pressure of the rest of the form.

This type of lid can be made on any scale.

283–286

287–289

The easiest way for showing the types of lid made upside down is in conjunction with a practice not so far described.

Throwing small forms from a large lump of clay

Small forms can be thrown from the top of a large piece of centred clay

290 The initial process is to slightly separate a ball of clay

291, 292 This is then opened up and thrown in the normal way

Forms thrown in this way can be removed in a number of ways.

293, 294 With the wheel revolving slowly a flat broad ended tool such as an old ruler is pushed towards the centre of the wheel under the thrown form. The operation can be timed so the ruler reaches the centre just as the wheel stops. Possibly also supported by the left hand the form can be lifted off the wheel onto a bat

295–302 Domed or flat lids, with or without flanges, may be thrown in this way

Forms thrown on a hump of clay can be cut off with a wire and lifted off but they can also be taken off without any tool at all. For this they should be thrown on a thin stem of clay.

Pressure on the stem of clay should be inwards and downwards. Upward and inward pressure will distort the form of the lid. When the clay stem becomes thin it will break and the lid can be lifted off onto a bat. The wheel should revolve only slowly for this process.

An advantage which can be taken when throwing lids upside down is to throw the whole of the under surface. It is often difficult to relate the thrown surface of a pot with a turned lid. Knobs can be thrown on in the techniques described in Section 12. When turned surfaces are being used the lid should be removed from the hump of clay with sufficient clay to allow a knob to be turned.

Section 9

Centring and opening large pieces of clay

The centring and opening of large pieces of clay is in principle no different to that of smaller pieces. But unless it is done methodically it can be exhausting and if it is done badly it can make the clay difficult to throw.

303 After wedging or kneading, which ideally immediately precedes throwing, the clay should be beaten into an even shape with a

convexity for its base and should be placed centrally on a dampened bat. It should not be thrown down—this does not make it stick any better and can damage the wheel bearings

304 The clay is then beaten into a conical form revolving the wheel slowly. The more care with which this is done the easier it will be to finally centre the clay

305 Both hands push on the lowermost part of the clay. Maximum force can be used if the whole body leans against the clay; the arms transfer the weight of the body and steady it by resting firmly on the edge of the wheel tray. With experience, maximum speed is usually preferred but beginners do sometimes find that this exaggerates eccentricities and when this happens a slower speed should be used

306 As the lower section becomes centred the hands move up to the uncentred section above working up the form all the time moving unevennesses upwards. In both these first two photographs of centring only inward pressure is being applied

307 With the whole of the lower section of the clay centred and with the left hand resting on the centred clay the right, linked to the left for steadiness, pushes down and in on the uncentred top of the cone to which the unevennesses of the lower parts have been removed

308 Once the top is centred the whole form should be centred and the hands can pivot downwards adjusting the form of the clay. No upward movement should be made when a lower point is off centre—in practice the left hand can push steadily on centred clay while the right hand, in a higher position, centres uneven clay.

There are other ways of centring large pieces of clay but this in practice is probably the easiest. Off-centre clay being moved from the point of most mass and therefore most resistance, the base, to the point of least mass and therefore least resistance, the top. If the opposite is tried the truth of this will be appreciated—centring is possible, but more difficult and tiring.

Adjusting the clay into a wider mass and opening it out can be one continuous combined operation

309, 310 The left hand pushes steadily on the side and contains the outward movement of the clay effected by the greater downward pressure of the right hand. The fingers of the right hand firmly grip the back of the left hand. The left forearm can rest on the wheel tray edge throughout this operation

311 When the form has reached its intended width the left hand prevents further outward displacement of clay by increasing its inward pressure and the wrist and palm of the right hand push downwards and outwards. The fingers of the right hand remain braced on the back of the left hand throughout this action.

If the actions in this process have been done faultlessly no unevenness should be seen in the rotating wall. Slight general eccentricity may be created by a slip and this can be steadied by removing the hands and pushing firmly but not too forcibly inwards on the nearest part of the wall with both palms, resting the fingers on the top of the wall and, depending on its size, inside, to steady it

312 Finer adjustments to the inside form created by the wrist can be done with the fingers of both hands. The form being thrown will obviously determine the exact nature of the form of the base

313, 314 Initial thinning can be done between the left hand fingers and the right hand palm, the hands interlocked for steadiness.

An alternative method of initial thinning of large forms is one of the very rare occasions when the right hand is used inside the form against the rotation of the wheel

315, 316 The hands move upwards quite normally. The clay is squeezed between the fingers of the right hand and the palm of the left. In this method the clay is revolving into the hands and pressure effected on the clay is considerably greater than normal.

Once the walls are fairly thin this method is too fierce to be easily controlled. One upward movement against the wheel is a quick way of beginning a wall and is usually sufficient

Section 10

Flat forms

The technique of making flat forms has not been shown on a small scale largely because flat forms such as plates and dishes are in fact simply horizontally extended versions of other forms and because the problems of the technique are perhaps easier to show on a large scale.

Plates and dishes usually have fairly flat bases and an edge form which varies. In dishes the edge form can be vertical or inward sloping or convex or concave in profile. The technique for making such forms is simply to throw the intended wall form on the widest point of a wide, flat centred piece of clay, the wall being thrown as described in Section 6. In plates the edge most usually flares outwards and the technique for making the edge wall of plates is closely similar to that of making other open forms. On a small scale flat forms should be easy and are good exercises for learning to control the thickness left in the opening up process.

On a larger scale some problems may arise.

The initial problem is in spreading out the centred piece of clay and opening it out without trapping slip or clay in the wall or base. Spreading out should be done with the edge at a shallow angle and with some pressure constantly on it so that any tendency to mushroom out and over is eliminated. A greater problem is in moving clay out from the centre of the mass to its edge during

the shaping of the base without creating a secondary wall of clay which might tend to fold over trapping slip and clay.

317 Two ways of doing this are possible. Downward outward pressure is here spread out over a considerable part of the radius. The side of the right hand is the point of maximum pressure, lesser pressure is exerted by the fingers of the left hand where displaced clay might tend to rise up into a wall

318 An alternative method and one that perhaps offers finer control is to spread the pressure over a radius using the finger tips. The finger nearest the centre pressing hardest and the others progressively less hard. Several outward movements in this manner can move a considerable amount of clay with considerable control

319 Once the flat supported inside form has been made the wall can be thinned

320 For almost all forms it should be thinned fairly vertically

321 When thinned the wall can be taken out to about 45 degrees in a form with an inside concavity

322 From this point probably only one further complete shaping action will be possible. To be effective this has to be as definite as possible

323 Stability of the whole edge form is relatively assured while the actual edge is still bent upwards

324 The very edge should be the last part affected by the shaping action. Once it has been flattened further shaping to almost any of the edge form would almost certainly lead to a complete loss of control and to collapse

325 A light trimming helps in centring the form before turning and in locating the wire during cutting off

Edge forms on plates when as thinly thrown and as flat as this do tend to curl up in drying. This can be arrested by drying the form very slowly but is difficult to prevent entirely.

A wheel with a very steady slow speed is essential for this type of form. The centrifugal force present but slight when throwing forms of smaller diameter becomes much more noticeable when forms of wider diameter are thrown.

Some clays are virtually impossible to throw thinly into this type of form and forms may sometimes have to be made almost solid with clays of poor throwing quality.

Dish forms where the edge form is much more vertical are much simpler forms to throw and even beginners should find them easy.

The qualities of the edges of all flat forms, whether they are classed as dishes or plates are very variable.

When flat forms with flat edges are being thrown fairly firm clay should be used.

Large flat forms are almost impossible to throw without the use of removeable bats. Large flat forms thrown on bats usually have to be removed from the wheel to be easily and safely cut off with a wire. The behaviour of a wire when such forms are cut off is of considerable importance. In whichever of the possible techniques cutting off is done, the clay left sticking to the bat will, as usual, be of negligible thickness at the edge but may be over $\frac{1}{4}$ in. thick in the middle. This means that bases have to be thrown fairly thickly but it also means that if a form is lifted off the bat before it is rigid and is placed on a flat surface the base will sink to a form other than that in which it was thrown. Where an inside base form is intended to be other than flat the whole form should be allowed to reach a turnable hardness before it is lifted off the bat. When a flat inside base is wanted (and perhaps no turning envisaged) if the base is thrown to a convexity known, by experience, to correspond with the convex form of the clay left on the bat, the hardened form can be lifted off the bat before it is rigid and the base, which will be even, can be pushed down flat.

Section 11

Throwing on a large scale

Throwing on a large scale is for many people one of the most interesting and challenging aspects of throwing. As a technique throwing is more limited than most techniques of making objects in the size of form it can produce. To many, making thrown forms as big as possible is a challenge. But this challenge does not exist for all.

Relatively little space is given to throwing large forms not because it is thought to be unimportant —far from it—but simply because it is not technically dissimilar from throwing smaller forms.

The difficulties which people imagine might exist in throwing large forms probably do not exist. The difficulties which are encountered by those who try are invariably difficulties created by the incomplete understanding of techniques which have not been fully learned on a smaller scale.

Faults which develop in large forms are proportionately bigger and more disastrous than the same faults in smaller forms. Sometimes faults latent in a small form will not develop simply because the form is small: in a large form the same fault will, apparently inexplicably, suddenly be present. Anyone with any experience of throwing knows when throwing is, technically, going well. Equally they know when, through a sudden slip or jolt they are responsible for a form becoming eccentric and uncontrollable. The faults in throwing which develop, apparently inexplicably, are invariably due to inadequate preparation of clay or to a fault in centring or opening up.

Providing clay is conscientiously prepared and providing throwing is methodically approached making large forms should be no more difficult than making smaller forms. And it hardly requires more strength In all throwing it is the intelligent application of pressure which matters; the amount of sheer strength available is largely irrelevant.

Some basic considerations can be usefully stated without going into the details of forms found in Section 6.

It is absolutely essential that a wheel on which large forms are to be thrown should have easily maintained slow steady speeds. As centrifugal force increases at increased radii the speed needs to be less than the speed for throwing smaller forms.

Clay for throwing large forms needs to be considerably firmer than that convenient for throwing smaller forms.

With many types of form considerably more taper will be necessary in the walls than when throwing small forms. All walls will of necessity be somewhat thicker than those of small forms.

Open forms

326 Initial thinning should be in even rising actions. Once a wall is at all thin the same parts of the hands, depending on preference, are used as when throwing small forms

327 In both thinning and shaping the relative positions of the hands are the same as when making smaller forms

328 Forming edge details and lightly trimming the base are the final action.

Fairly vertical, open shapes such as this can be thrown, if wanted, so that they need only slight turning.

Somewhat flatter open forms will need to be thrown on bases of sometimes considerable width. The necessary minimum base width for throwing a bowl of a certain diameter will vary from clay to clay and depends too on the type of form and the consistency of the clay used

329 The inside form of the solid base area must be determined before extensive thinning of the wall begins

330 The nature of the edge should be created at an early stage

331 The most difficult problem in throwing open forms is preventing the formation of an unintended convexity in the inside form of the bowl where the supported base stops and the unsupported wall begins. Once it has occurred it is difficult to remove. During both thinning and shaping it is an idea to reverse the usual position of the hands and to work on this part of the form with the right hand inside and the left palm supporting the wall outside. By doing this it is easier to see what one is doing. The reason the bump occurs is that the considerable pressure which can be exerted on the supported base is not reduced quickly enough when the wall is reached and the wall is pushed down leaving a bump. The only possible remedy is to push down on the bump. Pushing up on the wall invites a total loss of control. It is wrong in fact to have to make adjustments to the supported base, the form of which should be determined at the opening out stage. Only the walls should in fact have pressure applied to them. Forming the unsupported walls into an uninterrupted continuation of the supported base is one of the main problems in throwing large open forms

332-334 Thinning is done to a progressively wider form. The edge should be held and lightly compressed at the end of each upward action

335 Final shaping, involving no positive thinning, will increase the width and decrease the height slightly

336 Providing all actions have been controlled the form will be perfectly true and, if this is wanted, there should be no difficulty in smoothing the edge with a chamois leather

337 Turning of such forms will inevitably be necessary at least to some extent

338 When one has spent considerable time and effort preparing the clay for throwing, removing a form from its chuck during turning to feel its thickness, even doing this several times, is a sensible precaution

339 When turning is finished the form should be removed and handled with considerable care as its loss of thickness may make it less rigid than it seemed before.

One problem which may arise during the throwing of flat forms and open forms is that the outside becomes dry. Encountering a dry patch during thinning or shaping can easily drag a form off centre

340 The easiest way to dampen the outside of flat and open forms is to touch the outside of the wall near the top with the tips of the fingers and to squeeze water on to the palm of the hand. This will run down the fingers and on to the underside of the form

Section 12

Tall forms

Tall forms obviously fall into a number of loosely defined categories, infinite variety being possible within each one.

When clay of any reasonable throwing quality is being used it should be possible to throw tall forms without any need for subsequent turning unless they widen very quickly at a shallow angle near the base. Turned surfaces may obviously be preferred even when a form can be thrown without turning.

341 Initial thinning is most easily done into a fairly vertical form

342 Further thinning should be closer to the intended form. It should be possible to thin even the largest of forms in about four upward movements. Slight further thinning can take place during subsequent shaping actions

343, 344 Providing the form has been soundly thinned and the clay was well prepared shaping should be easy and quite considerable adjustments to form should be possible.

When throwing tall forms with fairly narrow tops it is important that the left forearm does not push out at the top of a form when thinning or shaping is being done lower down. Some stable form of block or a wide stool should be available to stand on so that this does not occur. It is as well to wet the left forearm so that if it does touch the top it does not drag on it

345 After each upward movement during both thinning and shaping the edge should be steadied

346, 347 Providing pressure is initially applied gently the upper parts of a form can be adjusted without starting each shaping movement right at the bottom of the form

136

Collaring, basically the same as that described on conical forms in Section 6, can also be done on tall forms.

The form should not be thinned too much in the part being collared but the shaping should be finished up to the point of collaring or certainly from only a very short distance below it.

348 The initial action in collaring is to bend the top of the form inwards. This minimises any tendency to folding as the narrowing pressures of collaring reach it

349–351 The thumb and index fingers then encircle the form, moving upwards

352 The collared section can then be thinned

353 Slight shaping of narrow topped forms is possible without any supporting pressure inside, though a long rib could be used. Pressure should be gentle, adjustments only slight and the top should be steadied throughout the action

354 It is perfectly possible to completely enclose such forms. Equally they can be thinned in an upward direction. The top should not be thrown to a considerably lesser thickness than the main part of the walls of a form

One tendency to be avoided in throwing larger forms is to overthin the top sections. This is easy to do but makes the clay damper and hence liable to greater shrinkage. In shrinking the proportions of the form change, sometimes considerably.

Some forms which can be made with relative ease on a small scale are sometimes much more difficult on a large scale. Very narrow tall forms are, for example, far from easy.

Throwing on a large scale is largely a matter of control and of experience. Both these develop with practice.

Section 13

Throwing in more than one stage

There are various techniques by which thrown forms can be added to by further throwing. These techniques, by which some of the most interesting forms in throwing can be made, open up a completely new range of possibilities, and are used for one of two main reasons. Forms are made which either because of their size or because of their nature are impossible to throw in one piece.

New forms can be thrown onto both the top and the bottom of previously thrown pieces.

Making thrown additions on the top of forms

(a) *Coiling and throwing*

Coiling and throwing has been largely used for making vast storage pots. Pots well over eight feet high have been made by this method. It can equally be used to throw forms which because of their nature could not be made in one piece. The technique is identical.

By far the most convenient method of doing coiling and throwing is to do it on removeable bats. After initial throwing the form should be cut off with a wire and immediately restuck by pressing on the base with the fingers and it should be kept restuck by sponging the untrimmed base. The clay of the initial stage should be dried slowly so that the edge is not too dry and the base not too damp. The clay should be firm but softer than the state at which it would be turned.

355 Initially the edge is scored and dampened with slip or water or both whichever is preferred

356 Then a thick evenly rolled out coil of even clay is placed on the top edge

357 The coil is then methodically fingered down on to the form

358 When the coil has been fingered down inside and outside and when the join in the coil has been worked over and fingered together, the form can be slowly revolved, pinching the wall up slightly and checking its evenness

359 Water is then sponged on to the coil as it is steadied—centred—between the thumb and fingers of the left hand

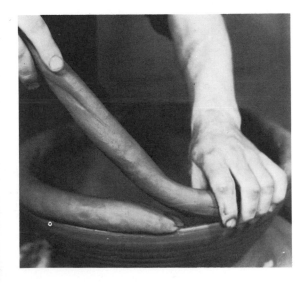

360 The coil can be thinned upwards in a perfectly normal manner. The edge should be firmly steadied. Sometimes it may be necessary to trim the top slightly but if the coil has been evenly made and evenly fingered onto the form this should be unnecessary

361, 362 The new wall can then be thrown outwards into a form which would not be possible on a thin open form thrown from one piece of clay

When very large forms are being made, each new wall developed from successive coils should not be made inappropriately thin for the size of the whole form.

Variations of the technique are possible. A much larger coil than shown can be added. Two or more coils can be added at a time provided they are well fingered together and pinched into a homogenous mass before any throwing begins.

Throwing should always be done in the minimum possible time so that the existing firm clay does not begin to soften and the new clay does not become too soft.

Being softer than the clay under it each successive addition tends to shrink inwards relatively more than the clay under it. This phenomenon has to be seen and experienced to be fully understood and adjustments to form can with experience be made to compensate for it.

Coiling and throwing can obviously easily be applied by one person to forms of any diameter.

(b) *Throwing a thick wall, lifting this on to a previously thrown form, and thinning the new wall*

363 This process begins in the same way as coiling and throwing. The cylinder here is firm but not very hard. Its top edge is scored and dampened

364 A thickly thrown wall of clay with a flaring edge inside and out is lifted on to the top of the firm form and carefully placed centrally.

This process is obviously easiest if removeable bats are used. The new form is thrown, lifted off the wheel on its bat, the firm form is replaced on the wheel and the new piece lifted into place on the prepared edge.

The new form is obviously a baseless thrown wall. Providing it is not thrown too thinly there should be no difficulty in handling it

365 The first action, and this should be done quickly, before any tendency to stick develops, is to grip the new wall between the hands, with the wheel revolving slowly, to centre it on the firm wall

366 As soon as it is centred and sticking has begun which will probably happen well inside one minute, the exterior flange at the base of the new wall should be thrown down on to the old wall with the right hand, supporting the old wall on the inside with the left hand. Some of the flange, the thin lower part, may become detached during this process—this does not matter at all

367 Next the inside flange of the new wall is pressed down with the left hand on to the old wall supporting the wall outside with the palm of the right hand.

It is irrelevant whether the inside or the outside flange is joined first what is very important is the supporting pressure of the other hand while joining is being done—the old clay should be just soft enough for there to be some risk of unsupported pressure distorting it

368 If the new form has become too wide at the top during joining or is a little eccentric it can be collared

369, 370 The new form can then be thinned in the normal manner. The protruding flange of joined clay can be safely removed with a wire or a metal kidney at any stage after thinning

371 Just as much control of shaping and of surface is possible as with normal throwing from a single piece of clay

As forms thrown in this technique may be of considerable scale—a form over three feet high thrown in a single additional stage is by no means unusual—something very firm on which to stand preferably of adjustable height, such as several large blocks, should be found before throwing is begun.

The new piece will shrink relatively more than the old. There is a limit to the width of soft clay one person can lift but if one or more helpers can be found this limit is obviously extended. Considerably greater successive increases in height can be achieved with this technique than with coiling and throwing but for forms of very wide diameter coiling and throwing is easier.

Coiling and throwing is usually done in quite a number of successive stages, lifting a thickly thrown wall on to a form and then throwing it can equally be done a number of times to make one large form. With both techniques care should be taken to see that the firm walls of a form are not excessively softened in the throwing of new sections at the top.

In both techniques if the form is very narrow some swaying of the whole form may begin after a certain height is reached when the top section is being thinned. The only remedy is for a second person to hold and steady the form near its middle. This problem excepted, either technique is limitless.

Joining together two leather-hard thrown forms

A leather-hard thrown form may be added either to the top or to the bottom of another leather-hard form. Whichever way the technique is used the visual problem of the relationship of the two forms probably poses more difficulties than the technical problem of joining them.

Joining an additional form on to the top of another form is technically mostly a problem of accuracy. The technique of joining them is identical to that used for joining a form on to the base of another form.

372 The inverted form, a fairly tall open form, is supported on the wheel in any of the ways normally used for turning and has been turned. Lines are turned lightly into its base corresponding with the diameter and thickness of the form being added. These grooves are dampened with water and slip

373 The additional form also scored and dampened is added and when the wheel has been revolved to check that it is centred it is pushed gently down until the slip emerges from the join. The edge of the additional form, if necessary, should have been turned to accommodate the curve of the inverted form.

The join can be left as an angular join. All that should be necessary is to clean the slip from the join with a wooden tool

374 If an angular join is not wanted the join should be scored and dampened and a coil of appropriate thickness can be applied

375 This coil should be fingered down and up on to both forms and the fingering evened while the wheel is slowly revolved

376 The coil can then be thrown effecting a more fluid join between the two forms

The use of a coil when the top of a form is being added to will usually be unnecessary but one can be used in the same technique.

Using the sticking process shown coils can be added to the sides of forms and thrown into ridges.

The advantage that joining two or more leather-hard forms together has over the other techniques described in this section is that, providing they are of the same consistency, the various parts are not subject to differing shrinkages.

The disadvantage is the difficulty of gauging the relationships of the various parts before they can be seen together.

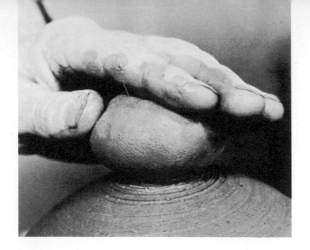

Throwing on to the base of leather-hard forms

Open forms are the most usual forms which are added to on their bases. It is equally possible to apply the technique to more enclosed forms. Any form which is being added to on its base is supported in exactly the same way as for turning and any necessary turning is done before the additional throwing.

(a) *Joining and throwing a ball of clay*

377 The intended extent of the base area of the thrown addition is scored and dampened. The ball of clay is applied and pressed down, twisting it slightly to help it to stick

378 The ball is evenly fingered down on to the leather-hard form

379 It is gently centred in the normal way

380 It is opened up

381, 282 The wall is then thrown into the intended form

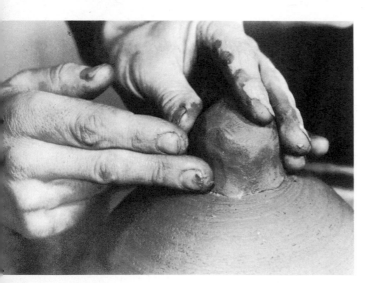

(b) *Joining and throwing a thrown wall of clay*
This technique is closely similar to that described for adding on to the top of forms.

383 The inverted leather-hard form has been prepared in an identical way to that used in the previous method but the scoring and dampening does not need to extend to the centre as the wall being added has no base. The soft wall should be thrown immediately before use and should flare out slightly inside and outside at the bottom

384 Immediately it is in position, and the scoring can be used as a rough guide, the wall is gripped lightly to centre it. It will not be easily moveable for much more than thirty seconds so this must be done quickly

385 The inside flange is pushed down gently on to the leather-hard form

386 The outside flange is then pushed down. This could be done before the inside, the order is unimportant

387, 388 The wall is then thrown into the intended form

With both these latter techniques while throwing is done quite normally care should be taken not to get too much water on the leather-hard form.

In some ways the second technique is the better. The pressure needed to centre the ball of clay may cause thinly turned forms to collapse. Being quicker, the second process is useful where relatively non-plastic clay bodies which tend to soften quickly are being used.

Both these techniques result in a type of shape usually called a stem form or a footed form. The fact that the stem part is thrown upside down and that the form cannot be seen right way up until it is leather-hard may initially be a problem. One can, of course, get some idea of what the form will look like by inverting one's head. Where enclosed forms are being added to, these will be partially hidden in a chuck and the visual problem here is much greater.

Where the second technique is used there is no reason why the new form should not be as big or bigger than the inverted form. The new form could in fact finally be the upper form in the finished object or the object could be reversible.

Both the fact that the final form is usually inverted and the fact that the new form shrinks relatively more than the old should, with experience, present no problems.

With stem forms it is as well to remember that the thrown foot form has to bear the weight of the total form both physically after firing and, perhaps more importantly, during firing and should for this reason neither have too thin an edge nor be too thin in its walls.

One of the first lessons usually taught to those using clay is that when clay is joined to clay the two parts should be of the same consistency. While the rule is an important one joined throwing is an exception to it. The possible tolerance between consistencies in differing clays should be quickly learned with experience. Once learned, if the techniques described in this section are conscientiously carried out the cracking away of additional thrown parts will not be a problem. Drying, however, should not be rushed.

Section 14

Mention of form so far has been almost entirely of a technical nature describing how procedures are varied when differing types of forms are made.

These technical considerations are basic, but more important considerations finally are the types, qualities and subtleties of forms which can be made. This brief last section is not an attempt to provide answers but simply to discuss some factors which sometimes influence these concerns.

Form, material and technique are inevitably inter-related and attached to every material and to almost every technique is its own scale of values—its own aesthetic.

Accepting that all materials and techniques possess their own particular and sometimes unique qualities it is true to say that each material and technique tends to produce objects of certain broad similarities or groups of objects of broad similarity. It is from within this range of qualities found that the particular and unique qualities can be seen. It is worthwhile making a personal attempt to classify these qualities to discover which are inherent in the material, which are inevitable in the technique, which, if any, are the result of conventional but variable or unnecessary details of technical procedure and which, if any, in either material or technique, are contrived.

Equally it is worthwhile seeing if objects can be made without contrivance by well tried techniques in well tried materials endowed with qualities other than those normally associated with those techniques and materials. From either or both of these experiments it will probably be found that some general qualities are the direct result of the use of a material and that some specific qualities are the result of either a specific technique or a detail of technique. Where some quality is the direct outcome of a detail of technique it is of some importance that the technique is chosen, rejected or altered consciously rather than used automatically because it happens to be part of a conventional procedure. The line of demarkation between good and bad use of material and technique is ultimately tenuous and debatable but it is pertinent and interesting to consider.

The texture of clay, the surface of a form, the scale of throwing or turning marks, the detailed form of edges, the nature of the base and, perhaps most important, the overall form of an object are factors relevant to the aesthetic of thrown form. They are all factors open to great variety some of which can stem directly from an individual's technique and most of which can be radically changed by intent. Clay can be turned into angular forms with hard precise surfaces characteristic of some techniques of metal working. It can be thrown into soft forms and turned to have granular qualities akin to stone. It can equally be thrown into light springing forms with softly rippled surfaces which have unmistakably a quality of clay thrown on a wheel. This last quality is an example of a unique quality of clay but the previous examples are other qualities with which clay can be endowed without contrivance.

While technique and material are far from unimportant it is ultimately the statement made through their use which is more important. The unique qualities of a material will not always be the most appropriate to a specific statement and every beginner should endeavour to become as much acquainted with the range of qualities of techniques and materials as with their unique qualities.

The rigidity of technical rules varies greatly from material to material. Hard materials that are difficult to work generally require a number of tools, each with a specific purpose. Specific tools usually need to be used in narrowly defined ways which tend to produce distinct and inevitable qualities. Plastic clay, in that it is soft and easily formable, can be thrown with few tools, or improvised tools or, excepting the wheel, no tools. Thus providing basic procedures are followed the technique and tools can be so considerably varied that no quality can be said to be inevitable except within the broadest of limits, broader than almost any other material. This width of quality in form and surface is possible partly because of the variation in the details of technique. Thinning and shaping a clay wall are done by the application of two simple pressures as they affect the revolving clay. This technique can be fairly quickly understood but the possibilities of the techniques of throwing can only be understood when it is realised how much the details of the technique can be varied. Beginners often assume the detailed position of the hands during a demonstration to be of absolute importance—it is only this if the aim is to make an identical object. An obvious concern of any thrower is to experiment with and explore form. An excellent complement to this is to experiment with and explore details of throwing technique—the speed of wheel rotation, the

speed at which the hands rise, the fingers which apply pressure to the clay, the angle of the fingers which apply pressure to the clay, the consistency of clay. It is only through a combination of and wide experiment with both intent and technique that the full possibilities of a technique can be realised.

The function of thrown form is, where it is relevant, an influence on the nature of form. What must be stressed is that function only determines the scale and the basic nature of the form. The former is often determined within narrow limits but the latter only ever within the broadest limits. Complete control can be exercised over the more detailed qualities of functional thrown objects.

When a material has been worked in a technique for a long time a tradition arises. Tradition is a strong influence in pottery in general and in throwing in particular. Its influence is inescapable—no one can claim to be unaffected by it—a total rejection of it is as much an affirmation of its strength as a total acceptance. Whatever is understood by it, and interpretations vary considerably it is too often quoted or accused and too rarely understood in the light of the work from which it arose. Even from a brief study, the history of pottery can be seen to have been a gradual but constant evolution of ideas and forms—the great figures of the past were, in their time, the most daring innovators. Reaction to tradition is most likely to be balanced if it is made from a position of some knowledge of the work of the past and this knowledge is interesting if it covers more fields than just pottery. It will then be seen that in many periods of history, certainly in the most lively ones, the contemporary environment of objects in other materials and of stylistic ideas was of greater importance than the preceding work in clay.

That the present is more important than the past and that the past has lessons of relevance to the present are two important aspects of tradition. The thrower today is in a new relationship to society and now, perhaps more than at any other time, he is faced with a wide and varied range of possibilities. For this choice to be fully appreciated it is essential it is made from a deep knowledge of the wide range of forms and qualities which can evolve from the technique of throwing.

Suppliers in Great Britain

A product which seems good to one person may be quite inappropriate for someone else. Personal acquaintance with materials, tools and equipment is ultimately the only criterion by which to assess quality. Buying goods unseen, of whatever repute, is foolish.

Clays

Moira Pottery Co Ltd
Moira
nr Burton on Trent
Staffs

Potclays Ltd
Wharf House, Copeland Street
Hanley, Stoke-on-Trent

Watts, Blake & Bearn Ltd
Newton Abbot, Devon

Ferro (Great Britain) Ltd
Wombourne
Wolverhampton WV5 8DA

Fulham Pottery Ltd
210 New King's Road
London S.W.6

Harrison Mayer Ltd
Meir
Stoke-on-Trent ST3 7PX

Round asbestos bats
Bingley, Son and Follit Ltd
Millbank Works
Minerva Road
Lonon N.W.10

Wheels
W. Boulton & Co
Burslem, Stoke-on-Trent

Bernard Webber Ltd
Phoenix Works
Hanley, Stoke-on-Trent

Wheels and general pottery supplies
W. Podmore & Sons Ltd
Caledonian Mills
Shelton, Stoke-on-Trent

Wheels and general pottery supplies

Wengers Ltd
Etruria, Stoke-on-Trent

Plans for the Leach kick wheel

The Leach Pottery
St Ives, Cornwall

Leach wheels to order

Woodley's Joinery Works
Newton Poppleford, Devon

Taylor electric wheels and kick wheels

Associated Pumps (Potters Equipment) Ltd
73 Brittania Road
London S.W.6

Suppliers in the USA

General materials

Stewart Clay Co. Inc
133 Mulberry Street
New York, NY 10013

Jack D. Wolfe Co. Inc
Brooklyn, NY

Craftools Inc
401 Broadway
New York, NY

Sculpture House Inc
38 East 30 Street
New York, NY 10016

Newton Potter's Supply Inc
96 Rumford Avenue
West Newton, Massachusetts 02165

Duncan Ceramic Products Inc
P.O. Box 7827
Fresno, California 93727

Bell Ceramics Inc
Box 697
Clermont, Florida 32711

Throwing wheels

Gilmour Campbell
14258 Maiden
Detroit, Michigan 48213

Randall Wheel
Box 531
Alfred, NY

J. T. Abernathy
212 South State Street
Ann Arbor, Michigan

Paul Soldner
Aspen, Colorado

Advanced Kiln Co
2543 Whittier Boulevard
Los Angeles, California

A. D. Alpine Inc
11837 Teale Street
Culver City, California

Skutt and Son
Box 202
Olympia, Washington.

Kilns

Unique Kilns
530 Spruce Street
Trenton, New Jersey

Dickinson Kilns Inc
2424 Glover Place
Los Angeles, California

Denver Fire Clay Co
3033 Black Street
Denver, Colorado

Clays

Edgar Plastic Kaolin Co
Edgar, Putnam County, Florida

A.P. Green Refractories Co
1018 East Breckenridge Street
Mexico, Missouri 65265

George Fetzer Co
1205 17th Avenue
Columbus, Ohio 43211

Kentucky-Tennessee Clay Co Inc
Box 447, Mayfield, Kentucky 42066

Bell Clay Co
Gleason, Tennessee 38229

Harris Clay Co
Box 429
Spruce Pine, North Carolina 28777

Cedar Heights Clay Co
50 Portsmouth Road
Oak Hill, Ohio 45656

Georgia Kaolin Co
433 North Broad Street
Elizabeth, New Jersey 07207

Other equipment

Simpson Mix-Muller Division
National Engineering Co
Suite 2060, 20 North Wacker Street
Chicago, Illinois 60606

Amaco (American Art Clay Company)
4717 West 16th Street
Indianapolis, Indiana 46222

Patterson-Ludlow Division
Banner Industries Ltd
1250 Saint George Street
East Liverpool, Ohio 43920

J. C. Steele and Sons Co
710 South Mulberry Street Drawer 951
Statesville, North Carolina 28677

Jamar Walker Corp, Inc
365 South First Avenue
East Duluth, Minnesota 55802

Ohaus
29 Hanover Road, Florham Park
New Jersey 07932

Brodhead-Garrett Co
4560 East 71st Street
Cleveland, Ohio 44105

Index

References are to the more important technical mention of the subjects.